Includes CD-Rom in pocket

THE
COMPLETE
IDIOT'S
GUIDE®

Personal Finance
Workbook

D1552276

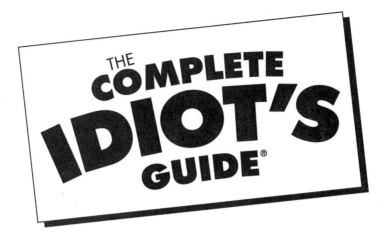

THE COMPLETE IDIOT'S GUIDE®

Personal Finance
Workbook

by John Napolitano, CPA, PFS, CFP

ALPHA

A member of Penguin Group (USA) Inc.

ALPHA BOOKS

Published by the Penguin Group

Penguin Group (USA) Inc., 375 Hudson Street, New York, New York 10014, USA

Penguin Group (Canada), 90 Eglinton Avenue East, Suite 700, Toronto, Ontario M4P 2Y3, Canada (a division of Pearson Penguin Canada Inc.)

Penguin Books Ltd., 80 Strand, London WC2R 0RL, England

Penguin Ireland, 25 St. Stephen's Green, Dublin 2, Ireland (a division of Penguin Books Ltd.)

Penguin Group (Australia), 250 Camberwell Road, Camberwell, Victoria 3124, Australia (a division of Pearson Australia Group Pty. Ltd.)

Penguin Books India Pvt. Ltd., 11 Community Centre, Panchsheel Park, New Delhi—110 017, India

Penguin Group (NZ), 67 Apollo Drive, Rosedale, North Shore, Auckland 1311, New Zealand (a division of Pearson New Zealand Ltd.)

Penguin Books (South Africa) (Pty.) Ltd., 24 Sturdee Avenue, Rosebank, Johannesburg 2196, South Africa

Penguin Books Ltd., Registered Offices: 80 Strand, London WC2R 0RL, England

International Standard Book Number: 978-1-59257-867-2
Library of Congress Catalog Card Number: 2008943863

11   10   09   8   7   6   5   4   3   2   1

Interpretation of the printing code: The rightmost number of the first series of numbers is the year of the book's printing; the rightmost number of the second series of numbers is the number of the book's printing. For example, a printing code of 09-1 shows that the first printing occurred in 2009.

Printed in the United States of America

Note: This publication contains the opinions and ideas of its author. It is intended to provide helpful and informative material on the subject matter covered. It is sold with the understanding that the author and publisher are not engaged in rendering professional services in the book. If the reader requires personal assistance or advice, a competent professional should be consulted.

The author and publisher specifically disclaim any responsibility for any liability, loss, or risk, personal or otherwise, which is incurred as a consequence, directly or indirectly, of the use and application of any of the contents of this book.

Most Alpha books are available at special quantity discounts for bulk purchases for sales promotions, premiums, fund-raising, or educational use. Special books, or book excerpts, can also be created to fit specific needs.

For details, write: Special Markets, Alpha Books, 375 Hudson Street, New York, NY 10014.

Publisher: *Marie Butler-Knight*
Editorial Director: *Mike Sanders*
Senior Managing Editor: *Billy Fields*
Senior Acquisitions Editor: *Paul Dinas*
Development Editor: *Lynn Northrup*
Senior Production Editor: *Megan Douglass*
Copy Editor: *Emily Garner*

Cartoonist: *Steve Barr*
Cover Designer: *Bill Thomas*
Book Designer: *Trina Wurst*
Indexer: *Celia McCoy*
Layout: *Ayanna Lacey*
Proofreader: *Laura Caddell*

Contents at a Glance

Contents

Introduction

If you're feeling a bit reluctant about jumping into the nuts and bolts of managing your personal finances, let me take a minute to help you relax. In fact, managing your money is a very freeing act. You no longer have to dread looking into your mailbox during those "special times" of the month or wait nervously while merchants run your credit card through the scanner. You're in charge—you know what you have, what you need, and where you're going.

The Complete Idiot's Guide Personal Finance Workbook will help you gain that freedom. It's not designed to teach you everything you need to know about personal finance. (For that, I'd recommend that you pick up a copy of *The Complete Idiot's Guide to Personal Finance in Your 20s & 30s, Fourth Edition*, by Sarah Young Fisher and Susan Shelly; see Appendix B.) This workbook does three things:

1. It gives you some basic facts about the major topics and tasks involved in managing your personal finances.

2. It offers you interactive worksheets, lists, tables, and other tools to help you manage your finances.

3. It explains why, when, and how you should use those tools.

I've worked hard to keep these tasks easy. Every worksheet in the book is included on the CD, so you can access them in fully interactive form. Plug in your information, calculate, revise, recalculate—the forms are yours to use again and again, and to adapt to your changing situations and needs.

This is a workbook, and I've kept the information tightly focused on the job of getting your financial house in order. I don't assume that you particularly enjoy the subject of financial planning (not as much as I do, anyway), so I won't take up your time with any "fascinating facts" that don't actually help you accomplish anything. Time is money, after all, and this workbook is all about helping you get the most out of your money—and your life.

What You'll Find in This Book

I've organized this book into four major parts:

Part 1, "Getting Started," covers the necessary first steps down the path toward financial freedom—determining where you are financially, where you want to go, and what you need to do in order to jump-start the journey. This is where you stare all of your financial realities in the face and then make them start answering to you. By the time you finish the worksheets in this part of the book, you'll know what you own, what you owe, and where your current spending habits are taking you. You'll have your financial plan in place, a workable budget to match that plan, and a safe and efficient setup for all of your financial records. Not bad, for starters.

Part 2, "Managing Expenditures," shows you how to keep a lid on your cash out-flow, from planning major purchases to managing your debt and protecting your assets. You learn how to plan for buying or renovating a home, fund a vacation, wrestle your credit card debt into submission, compare insurance policies and benefits, and how to protect your precious cache of growing assets. You also get (and learn how to usc) some powerful tools for making sure that you don't pay more on your taxes than you rightfully owe—a goal all of us share.

Part 3, "Accumulating Wealth: Savings and Investment," shows you some simple and savvy techniques for pumping up your monetary inflow. After a short trip through some savings and investment basics, these chapters help you determine the best invest-ment choices for your circumstances and goals. You learn how to track and manage your current investments, and how to maintain a successful investment strategy as your assets and income grow (and believe me, they will).

Part 4, "Planning for the Future," looks down the road to help you plan for the more financially successful future you're learning to build. You learn how to use some important tools for making sure that your financial future is everything you want it to be. From saving for your children's (or grandchildren's) college education, to planning and funding your retirement, and beyond, the tools you gain in these final chapters will help you and your loved ones stop worrying about tomorrow, so you can focus on today. We wrap up the workbook with some tools and guidance for staying on track when your financial situation changes, and determining when you need to call in the outside help of a qualified financial professional.

And, just so we don't leave you hanging, we've included a glossary and a list of resources that you can use to learn more about any of the topics or tasks we cover in the workbook.

Extras

As you work through this book, you'll find three types of sidebars, designed to help you in your progress:

In the Know

These boxes offer inside advice about issues and decisions that can enhance the management of your personal finances.

Pitfall Alert!

These boxes caution you about time wasters, common missteps, tricks by financial vendors, regulations, or other sticky traps that could affect your finances.

def•i•ni•tion

These boxes define key words and phrases from the book's text.

How to Use the CD

The CD that accompanies this book contains all of the worksheets from every chapter. Some of these worksheets are highly interactive, with formulas and functions that you can return to frequently as your financial "facts" change over time. Others provide valuable checklists and other tools to help you keep your financial future on track.

Trademarks

All terms mentioned in this book that are known to be or are suspected of being trademarks or service marks have been appropriately capitalized. Alpha Books and Penguin Group (USA) Inc. cannot attest to the accuracy of this information. Use of a term in this book should not be regarded as affecting the validity of any trademark or service mark.

Part  Getting Started

You're ready to get a handle on your personal finances, but where do you start? Well, right here, of course! You're about to find out just how easy it can be to take charge of your financial life.

Are you working toward the day when you can pay off those student loans and own your education free and clear? Do you have your heart set on starting your own business and telecommuting from Tahiti? Are you determined to pay for your kids' college education, so they don't have to suffer under the brutalities of student loan payoffs, and then can start their own businesses and telecommute from Tahiti (rather than live in your basement)? Whatever your financial dreams involved, Chapters 1 through 4 of this book give you everything you need to start making them come true.

Chapter

1

Where Do You Stand?

In This Chapter

◆ Adding up your assets

◆ Owning up to what you owe

◆ Finding your net worth

◆ Making it all worthwhile

The first step toward a healthier and more prosperous economic future (and that's what this book is all about) is to take a calculated look at your current condition. What do you own? What do you owe? These are the questions we tackle in this chapter. By the time you've finished the work-sheets included here, you'll have a very clear and specific understanding of how your assets and liabilities stack up against each other to determine your net worth. You'll also have the tools you need to track your net worth—and your economic progress—over the years ahead.

Taking Stock of Your Assets

Your mother may have told you that your quick wit and dazzling smile are your greatest assets, but the chances are strong that you own a few things worth a bit more on the open market. If you have a job, you undoubtedly buy things occasionally, and some of those things may have even increased in value (such as your house or stock holdings). And, okay, a few of them may have already been chucked into the landfill (bye-bye, abdominal cruncher!). The only way to know the real value of your assets—both *financial* and *liquid assets*—is to list them all and add them up.

To begin, you need to have some information handy. Take a minute to gather up all of your bank statements, life insurance policies, and savings and investment account information, including:

- Your most recent checking and savings account balances
- Your current home mortgage, car, boat, and other loan values and payoff balances
- The most current value reports for any stocks, bonds, CDs, IRAs, or other retirement/pension accounts you might hold

If you have receipts or records of major purchases—computers, home entertainment systems, appliances, jewelry, cameras, antiques, and so on—have that information handy as well. If you have an appraisal of that coin collection you've been building since you were 10, grab it, too.

def•i•ni•tion

A **financial asset** is anything you own that can be sold or traded in for cold, hard cash. **Liquid assets** are those that involve funds—such as cash, checks, stocks, bonds, life insurance with cash-surrender value, IRAs, other retirement funds, and so on—that can be accessed in a day or two and cashed in for a specific payout amount.

Starting with the Big Stuff: Real Estate Holdings

For most of us, our home and other real estate—vacation cottages, business buildings, and so on—represent our largest assets. So, real estate offers a good place to begin your asset list. Use the Market Value Real Estate table to calculate the total current market value of every property you are invested in, whether as a sole owner/buyer or as a joint venture.

You don't need to pay for a real estate appraisal in order to approximate your property's current value. Check out Internet sites such as Zillow (www.zillow.com) or Yahoo's real estate site (http://realestate.yahoo.com/Homevalues) to learn about comparable property values in your area. Most major real estate company sites allow you to search for homes by zip code, number of bedrooms, square footage, and other qualifiers— another great way to find out what comparable homes in your area are going for.

Market Value Real Estate	
Property	**Market Value**
Primary Residence	$
Vacation Home	$
Business Building	$
Investment Real Estate	$
Other (list)	$
	$
	$
Total Market Value of Real Estate	**$**

Money in the Bank (and Elsewhere): Cash, Checks, and Investments

Now, it's time to account for your cash and "cashable" accounts. In this phase of your asset tally, add up the value of all of your cash, checks, investments, IRAs, and other retirement funds or 401K accounts in which you have a *vested equity*. You should also include the value of any life insurance policies you have that carry a cash-value balance. Use the Liquid Assets table to list and tally these assets.

def•i•ni•tion

Vested equity refers to savings or stock that is fully available to you within your employer's 401K plan, company stock ownership program, or other employee savings and investment plans. Most such plans require that you stay with the company for a period of time—usually years—before you are fully vested and thus have access to the full equity of your account.

```
Liquid Assets

Bank Accounts                    $ _____

Investment Accounts              $ _____

IRAs                             $ _____

Certificates of Deposit          $ _____

Life Insurance Cash Value        $ _____

Retirement Plans                 $ _____

Other (list)                     $ _____

                                 $ _____

                                 $ _____

Total Liquid Assets              $ _____
```

All This, and More: Valuing Your Personal Possessions

Life is about more than stocks, bonds, and cozy retirement plans—and so is your assets list. Here, take a moment to tally up the value of your personal possessions: your car, boat, household furnishings, jewelry, professional-quality camera, that massive lawn tractor with its own DVD player and global positioning system, and so on. All of these things have some monetary value, and therefore, should be included among your list of assets. Use the Value of Personal Possessions table to list and tally your personal possessions.

Don't stress over the details of this listing—you're simply trying to arrive at an approximate idea of what you could (gulp) sell your personal possessions for in the open market. For our purposes, you can limit your listings to those items worth $500 or more. Although you're unlikely to sell off your diamond necklace or home entertainment center, you could; and that fact earns them a spot in the assessment of your net worth.

Pitfall Alert!

Most IRAs and other retirement-savings accounts levy stiff penalties for early withdrawal. Those penalties reduce the accounts' current value—that's why you should consider these assets "untouchable" for anything but their intended purpose (or an extreme emergency).

Remember, what you paid for something may have little to do with its current value in the open marketplace. To get a good sense of that value, you can scan your newspaper's Classified section, troll through the appropriate sections of your area's online Craigslist (www.craigslist.org), or search through eBay's auction results for items similar to those you're valuing.

Value of Personal Possessions	
Automobile 1	$
Automobile 2	$
Household Furnishings	$
Electronics	$
Jewelry	$
Other (list)	$
	$
	$
Total Value of Personal Possessions	**$**

What You Owe: Adding Up Your Liabilities

Now that you've had an opportunity to consider just how much you own in this world, it's time to think about the other side of the coin (so to speak). Your net worth is the difference between the combined value of your assets and the total of your financial liabilities. So let's figure out just how much your liabilities amount to.

Yours, Mine, and the Bank's: Mortgage Debt

Again, we'll start with the big stuff. Use the Mortgage Debt table to list the amount of mortgage debt you carry for the real estate holdings you included in the Market Value Real Estate table shown earlier in the chapter.

Mortgage Debt

Property	Outstanding Debt
Primary Residence	$
Vacation Home	$
Business Building	$
Investment Real Estate	$
Other (list)	$
	$
	$
Total Mortgage Debt	**$**

What's Your Limit? Calculating Credit Card Debt

Okay, for some of us, this part of the calculation can be a bit painful. But don't be intimidated by the truth! If you charge little and pay off your balance every month, you're golden. If you're flailing around in the deep end of the credit card pool, you need to determine just how far you have to swim to reach safer waters. Use the Credit Card Debt table to list and total your credit card debt.

? In the Know _____

Remember to include every credit card with a current balance. In addition to the usual workhorses such as MasterCard and Visa, you may have a credit card balance with a home improvement store, furniture store, clothing store, or other frequent shopping destination.

Any Other Loans or Liabilities?

You're almost finished digging around in your debt! Before you start your net worth calculations, though, you need to account for any other outstanding debt you might carry. Use the Other Loans and Liabilities table to record the outstanding balance of any home equity loans, car loans, student loans, or other debts that you currently are paying in installments.

Credit Card Debt

Credit Card   **Outstanding Debt**

$ _____

$ _____

$ _____

$ _____

$ _____

$ _____

$ _____

Total Credit Card Debt   **$ _____**

Other Loans and Liabilities

Loan/Liability   **Outstanding Balance**

$ _____

$ _____

$ _____

$ _____

$ _____

$ _____

$ _____

Total Loans/Liabilities   **$ _____**

You don't need to list alimony or child support payments you make each month as liabilities. These payments will be accounted for in your budget—which we create in Chapter 3.

The Moment of Truth: Calculating Your Net Worth

Okay, you've done the heavy lifting. Now it's time to see just what kind of a financial nest egg you're sitting on. Use the Net Worth Calculator table to plug in and tally up the values you've calculated in previous sections of this chapter.

Net Worth Calculator
Bill & Mary Gill
Statement of Assets & Liabilities
December 31, 2008

Assets	Balance
Bank Accounts	$
Investment Accounts	$
IRAs	$
CDs	$
Life Insurance Cash Surrender Value	$
Retirement Plans	$
Market Value of Real Estate	$
Value of Personal Possessions	$
Family Business	$
Total Assets	$

Liabilities	Balance
Mortgage Debt	$
Credit Card Debt	$
Other Loans	$
Family Business	$
Total Liabilities	$
Total Net Worth (Assets - Liabilities)	$

Why Knowing Your Worth Is Worthwhile

So how much are you worth, anyway? Unless you're running in all of the wrong circles, no one will actually *ask* you that question, but it's important information for you to know. Maybe you're happily surprised at just how much your hard-earned property and possessions are worth. Maybe you're shocked that you don't have more to show for all of that "hard earning" you've been doing. In either case, you know exactly where you stand financially, and that's essential for determining where you want to go.

Remember, your net worth will change over time—and it's certain to improve with the sound advice and helpful tools you've scored in this book. By tracking your net worth, year after year, you can follow your financial progress and determine just how successful your personal financial planning has been. You'll know when you're on the right financial path, and when you're straying dangerously close to the snake pit of financial distress. Most importantly, you have a solid starting point for mapping out a plan for achieving your financial goals— and that's just what you're going to do in the next chapter of this book.

In the Know

Be sure to hang on to your net worth calculations and the information you gathered to complete them. You'll be compiling more detailed listings of these assets and liabilities when we talk about financial record-keeping, managing investments, retirement planning, and other long-range aspects of personal finance later in this book.

The Least You Need to Know

- ◆ Your net worth is the total value of your financial assets, minus the total value of your financial liabilities.

- ◆ In calculating your financial assets, you need to count the current market value of your assets, not the amount you originally paid for them.

- ◆ IRAs and other retirement accounts may be worth considerably less if you withdraw from them prematurely. Learn about potential penalties before withdrawing money from these accounts.

- ◆ Track your net worth from year to year, to determine how successfully your financial plan is working.

Chapter 2

Where Are You Going?

In This Chapter

- Building a map for your future
- Important questions to ask yourself
- Putting the milestones in place
- Making it happen

After you've determined just where you stand in the world of personal finance—what you own, what you owe, and how the two groups stack up against each other—it's time to take a long, critical look down the road ahead. You work to earn money, so you can use that money to create the best life possible. But when was the last time you stopped to think exactly what that "best life" would be like?

In the day-to-day hustle of working, paying bills, managing a household, and enjoying (or at least trying to enjoy) a semi-active social life, it's easy to forget that all of this is leading you somewhere. It's called "the future." Now, you don't have to plan for this trip. You're guaranteed to arrive at some kind of future, whether you follow a carefully detailed itinerary, or simply sleepwalk through life. You're reading this book, so it's safe to assume that you want to have some say-so in what your future entails. That means you have to decide what kind of future you want and how you're going to make that future happen.

That's the essence of financial planning and the purpose of this chapter. Here, you learn some simple techniques for purposeful dreaming, as you give thought to the future as you would like it to be. Next, the chapter's worksheets help you flesh out that dream through setting specific goals and determining objectives for achieving them. Finally, you build your master plan for putting your ideas into action. Remember, we're talking about *your* life, *your* dreams, and *your* money. Here, in the planning stage, is where you begin to take control of all three.

Designing the Dream

The first step in getting your financial future together is taking a moment to think about and acknowledge the things that matter most to you about your life. Whatever your dreams of an ideal life might encompass, you can achieve them only if you make a decision to do so. As often as your teachers may have told you to quit daydreaming, here, I encourage you to indulge in that happy pastime. In this section, you get a chance to listen to what your heart and mind are telling you about the life you'd like to live. With this information in mind, you'll be much better able to build a plan for your own best future.

 In the Know _____

If the idea of following your dreams seems a bit too new-agey and unsubstantial, reframe the idea as envisioning your future. Whatever you call it, forming and retaining a clear vision of the personal and financial future you want to inhabit can help guide you toward achieving it. This isn't any metaphysical secret; it's simply the way the human mind works.

Asking the Important Questions

Chances are, you haven't spent much time thinking about the kind of future that you'd most like to experience. Now is the time to do just that. Ask yourself the following questions to imagine the way you want your life to be. Jot down your answers, then come back and redo the questionnaire again next week, next month, next year. (You might want to make several copies of these questions before you fill in your answers.) These are "big picture" questions, and your answers to them might change over time. Right now, however, they form the starting point from which you'll begin to determine just what it is that you're working toward in life.

I am most happy when I am _____

_____

_____

_____

My ideal day would include _____

_____

_____

_____

My ideal week would include _____

_____

_____

_____

My ideal year would include _____

_____

_____

_____

My ideal job would involve _____

_____

_____

_____

My ideal home would offer _____

_____

_____

_____

Determining Your Priorities

Great! The simple "ideals" you've just noted form the rough outline of the future you want to achieve. The next step is to consider how you prioritize the main categories of elements that go into each of those ideal scenarios. The Priorities Organizer can help you do that. Within each category, list the thing (or things) that matter most to you about that category. Then, use a scale of 1 to 5 to indicate how much satisfaction you expect to achieve from each category and the items you've listed within it.

Pitfall Alert! _____

Everything changes over time, and that includes ideas, dreams, and goals. So, don't tie a bow on your future and tuck it away on the closet shelf. Instead, return to the Important Questions list and the Priorities Organizer occasionally, so you can keep your vision of the future—and your commitment to achieving it—alive and growing with you.

This worksheet serves two purposes: it helps you understand more specifically what it is that matters most to you about the "big picture" issues in your life, and it helps you prioritize those issues, based on how much expectation for satisfaction you place on each category. There aren't any right answers here. You may well draw more satisfaction from a great social life than you will from landing your dream job; hopefully you know that about yourself before you decide whether to take the accounting gig in Pittsburgh, or apply for the manager's spot at that Surf Shop in Maui.

Identifying Your Strengths

You know the old saying, "What doesn't kill you makes you stronger?" Every ugly life lesson tossed your way has given you new strengths to tackle the challenges that lie ahead. Kicking yourself over past mistakes is a pointless practice. A much more powerful response is to use what you've learned in the past to create a better future. You can transform your previous weaknesses into new strengths, and use those strengths to help achieve your goals.

So now, before you set your personal and financial goals for the future, take a minute to remember the important strengths you've developed over the years. Use the Negative Experience to Positive Strength worksheet to assemble a list of the missteps that most haunt you—the messiest financial or personal potholes that you've stumbled across (or fallen into) in your life and what they've taught you. Jot down the essence of what went wrong in the situation, and then be sure to note what went right—how the experience changed your future actions, and how you expect those changes to improve your outcomes.

Priorities Organizer

Category	What's important to you about this category?	Satisfaction Rating (1-5, with 1 lowest to 5 highest)
Family	I want to raise my children near their extended family	4
Health	I want to get in shape--and stay that way!	3
Money	I want to double my current income within 5 years	5
Career		
Community		
Social Life		
Recreation		
Spirituality		
Anything Else?		

Negative Experience to Positive Strength				
Issue	*What Went Wrong*	*What Went Well*	*What I Would Do Differently Next Time*	*Expected Outcome*
Lost $ in 401k	Too much in company stock; not well diversified; failed to track performance	Heard the wake-up call; changed allocations	Know and respect my tolerance for risk; plan and monitor my asset allocation; rebalance my portfolio as necessary	Even out the "highs" and the "lows" in my portfolio performance

Setting Goals and Objectives

Okay, you've spent some time considering your broad hopes and dreams for the future, and the strengths you've developed for the journey. Now, it's time to think about the actual milestones along the way by setting some specific goals and objectives. These goals and objectives will become the framework for your life blueprint—the action plan for building your future.

Identifying Your Personal Goals

Even when we don't realize it, our personal and financial goals walk hand in hand. The single person who wants to find and marry a true love, the 30-something who wants to get back in shape, the unhappy worker who desperately wants to escape wage slavery—all of these folks will alter their financial future as they work to achieve their personal goals. That's why you need to keep *both* types of goals in mind when creating your life blueprint.

Use the Personal Goals and Objectives worksheet to build a list of your personal *goals* and your *objectives* for achieving them. Remember, what separates a goal from a dream is having a plan. In your first step toward designing that plan, be sure to list a date by which you want to achieve your goals and a few of the major steps—objectives—involved in the process. Finally, use the category descriptions at the top of the worksheet to identify just how critical (Must-have? Important-but-not-essential? Ultimate-dream-achievement?) each goal is to you.

def•i•ni•tion

Goals and objectives are two different beasts. In this book's context, a **goal** is the broad purpose you're working toward: "I want to own my own home." An **objective** is a specific step toward achieving a goal: "In three years, I want to have accumulated $20,000 toward a down-payment on a house."

Financial Goals and Objectives

Ah, yes, the nitty gritty. You've developed a relatively thorough idea of your dreams and the goals that go into them. But now it's time to get specific about *financing* your vision. Just how do you want to change your current financial situation? Beyond stumbling across a burlap bag stuffed with untraceable currency and precious stones, how do you see yourself funding your dreams? The answers and the methods for achieving them are many, but only *you* know which ones will work best for you.

The Financial Goals and Objectives worksheet will help you list and prioritize your financial goals. Read through the listed goals, and determine which of them match your own concerns. Don't care about paying for your grandkid's college education? Check the None column for that one. Has your cash flow problem become a tsunami? Then rank that concern as High. When you're finished checking (and adding your own) concerns, step back and take a look at the finished list. You'll have a clear indicator of the financial goals you must tackle, and their priority. You'll also see patterns in the strengths and weaknesses of your current approach to financial management.

Personal Goals and Objectives

Category 1: Items and activities in this category are those most dear to you, items that you must have – considered a **core need.**

Category 2: Items and activities in this category are those that would exceed your requirements for happiness and comfort – considered **desirable.**

Category 3: Items and activities in this category are those that would far exceed your best-case scenarios – considered a **wow.**

Goal or Objective	By When	Item or Activity Description	Category (core need, desirable, or wow)
Eat healthier food	Next month	Stop with the fast-food lunches; declare no-meat Mondays; shop at the farmer's market; make and freeze healthy meals on weekends; don't keep junk food in the house; think before eating	1!!
Organize my closets and throw out junk	September	Set aside 1 hour for the next four Saturdays to work on this; commit to no new clothes until finished; sort, toss, stack, repeat	2
Write and sell a screenplay	Before my 40th birthday	Write for 1 hour every night; take a course in creative writing/screenwriting; find an agent; have some exciting experiences, so I can work them into my storyline	3

Financial Goals and Objectives
ASSESSMENT FORM

	Concern		
	High	Low	None
Establishing a regular, systematic savings plan			
Managing cash flow			
Establishing an emergency reserve fund			
Developing or revising your investment strategy			
Minimizing personal income taxes			
Saving and investing for a comfortable retirement			
Establishing an IRA, SEP, or Keogh retirement plan			
Building funds for your children's education			
Building funds for your grandchildren's education			
Providing care for elderly parents			
Making gifts to relatives			
Making gifts to charity			
Minimizing your estate tax			
Determining how your estate assets are distributed			
Avoiding probate costs at death			
Minimizing the burden of health-care costs			
Providing for your family in the event of death			
Providing for your family in the event of disability			
Ensuring your insurance coverage is cost-effective			
Changing or modifying your career			
Saving for a major purchase or vacation			
Planning for a comfortable retirement			

Getting to "Success": Following an Action Plan

Your vision of the future is crystal clear. You've outlined your path and identified the major milestones along the way. Now, it's time to plan your trip. In this section of the chapter, we're going to draft a blueprint for success—your success!

How's That Working for You?

You're already enjoying some successes in your life, right? Maybe you've landed that job you wanted. Or you were finally able to move out of that studio apartment and now have a bedroom that doesn't share space with the kitchen sink. You might have paid off the bills for last winter's skiing trip, and it isn't even time to go again yet!

Your idea of success is yours and yours alone. Before you map out the action plan for your success, take a minute to consider the successes you've already achieved, and how you might leverage them into bigger and better things. The Success Meter worksheet will help you do that. List the things that are working for you now, how they fit into your definition of success, and then think about how you might use them as next steps to future successes.

Drafting Your Action Plan

You've had some practice in thinking about your dreams, priorities, goals, and objectives, and how you can leverage the successes you've already achieved. Now it's time to put it all together into one concrete Action Plan. This plan should form the blueprint of your life, and like a blueprint, it should be complete and detailed.

Gather all of the information you've recorded in the preceding worksheets in this chapter, and use that to fill in the Life Blueprint Action Plan. Try to list your goals in the order of their importance. Commit to a specific time-frame for completing them, and list the most important tasks and tactics you'll have to accomplish. Finally, make sure you acknowledge who will be responsible for achieving them.

Remember that drawing up an Action Plan for achieving your goals is an act of freedom. Rather than being controlled by money, you are taking the upper hand by determining how, why, when, and where you will distribute your hard-earned cash. When you're just starting down the road to financial freedom, "giving in"—buying that way-too-expensive leather coat, booking that last-minute winter getaway to St. Barts—might feel like a declaration of independence from financial drudgery. But when you don't have the funds to pay for occasional splurges, they just add to the ball-and-chain debt that holds you back from the good life. Following your Action Plan is the quickest and most reliable way to become *truly* free with your money. With obligations met and a reserve of cash on the side, you can wake up some February morning and decide, with no worry or pangs of guilt, "Maybe I'll go see what it's like in St. Barts this weekend."

Success Meter			
What Is Going Well For Me?	*Why Is That Good?*	*What Greater Success Can I Develop From This?*	*First Steps*
I was promoted to Assistant Manager	More money, more respect at work	Improves my resume; work toward further promotions or better job elsewhere	Get good review in October
Going to the gym regularly	Lost 12 pounds	Start training for mini-marathon	Increase time on treadmill; add 1-hour run, 3x per week

Life Blueprint Action Plan			
Goal	*By When*	*Tasks and Tactics*	*By Whom*
Pay off MasterChains charge card	June of this year	Freeze card in ice Eat out 1x a week only, and pay cash Limit online purchases to $50 a month	Me Me/Julie Me
Stop relying on bailouts from Mom and Dad	Now	Don't talk about money problems w/parents Agree that "gifts" are for gift occasions only Live within my means, so they don't have to worry about it	Me Me/parents Me

Tracking Your Action Plan Progress

When builders work on a major project, they rely on their blueprints for guidance. At various phases of the project, however, the construction managers keep tabs on the details by periodically checking off a "punch list" of progress. Your Action Plan is every bit as detailed as the construction of an office building, so it pays to stay on top of the details.

You can use the Action Plan Punch List to track the progress you're making on each of your goals. After writing in the specific goal and target date at the top of the worksheet, list each task and tactic you've identified as being necessary to accomplishing it. (This list may grow as you move forward.) Give every task and tactic a target date for completion, and then record the actual completion date. When you hit an obstacle, write it down, along with your best ideas for overcoming it. Obstacles may morph into additional goals—who knows? The important thing is that you're working your plan and taking charge of your life—and your financial future.

Action Plan Punch List				
Goal: **Buy a better car**				*Target Date:* **October 2010**
Tasks and Tactics to Accomplish Goal	*By When*	*Date Completed*	*Obstacle*	*Obstacle Action Plan*
Accumulate $5,000 for down payment	September 2010		Other bills; current car needs work ($)	Save $200 a month; add all money gifts to fund; take free car repair class at community center
Do research into best car/price	June 2010	July 2010	I want what I can't afford!	Look for used-car options w/more luxury for less $$

The Least You Need to Know

◆ Your financial future is just one element of the life you want to lead, so don't expect to "buy" a happy future.

◆ To create a clear vision of the future you're working toward, you need to consider your dreams, your priorities, and the goals and objectives that will help you achieve them.

◆ You already have developed a number of strengths that you can leverage in accomplishing your personal and financial goals. To know them is to use them!

◆ Create an Action Plan to list and tackle specific goals.

◆ Stay on top of your progress! Track obstacles and milestones for all major goals, and remember to occasionally update your goals to match your changing priorities and circumstances.

Cash Flow: Fueling the Engine of Your Dreams

In This Chapter

◆ How swift is your current cash flow?

◆ Building a bearable budget

◆ This is you, managing your cash!

◆ Preparing for the great (and not-so-great) unknown

In the world of personal finance, cash flow—money coming in, money going out—is what it's all about, baby. Managing your cash flow isn't just a matter of watching how much you spend. It's that and a lot more—getting the most bang for your buck, managing debt, building savings, and other acts of personal freedom. A budget is your primary and most powerful tool for managing your cash flow. The worksheets in this chapter help you put together a budget that will work as an effective and efficient cash-flow manager for years to come.

Whatever your dreams for the financial future might involve, your budget is your ticket to achieving those dreams. The budgeting tools in this chapter will help you manage your cash today and accumulate the funds you need for the major purchases—and "surprise" expenses—of tomorrow.

Determining Your Cash Flow

In Chapter 1, you calculated your net worth. Your net worth offers a snapshot of your current financial state, but it doesn't tell you much about how that picture developed. To get a close-up look at your personal finances, you need to focus first on how much money you have coming in, and where all of that money is going, day after day, month after month. You determine that information by tracking your cash flow.

Your Income: The Necessary Details

How much detail is necessary for determining your cash flow? Within reason, you need to account for all of the money that regularly makes its way into (and out of) your hot little hands. What's left at the end of that process is your *net income*. No, you don't necessarily have to add in that $5 bill your Great-Great Aunt Betty tucks into your birthday card each year, but don't forget to count in other periodic (and reliable) "extras," such as sales commissions, bonuses, CD interest, dividends, business or rental income, and so on.

After you've determined how much money lands in your hands, your next step is to create a very detailed record of where all those shiny pennies are rolling off to. If you haven't been collecting and storing records of your expenditures, start doing that right now, and continue for one month. Save every receipt, bill, and other record of your financial transactions. If you spend it, record it. Then, gather up all of your financial records—credit card bills and receipts—and use them to build an accurate image of your cash flow.

def•i•ni•tion

Your **net income** is your bottom line: the total amount of money you have coming in each month, minus the amount of money you spend each month.

Use the Net Income Analyzer to determine how much money you're pulling in and where it goes. Your pay stub will show all deductions from your gross pay, but don't forget to then add income from other sources, such as interest-paying accounts or dividends.

Money In, Money Out: Analyzing Your Cash Flow

Now, it's time to determine what all of this calculation has revealed. If you subtract your expenses from your net income, the remainder is your cash flow. So, for example, if you're bringing in $3,100 a month, and you're spending $2,800 in that same period, your cash flow is $300. If, on the other hand, you're spending $3,700 a month, your cash flow is –$600, and you're living in the red zone. Even if you're only a few dollars in the hole each month, that trickle of blood that's leaking out of your fiscal artery can become a hemorrhage before you know it.

Net Income Analyzer	
Gross Income	**$2,450**
Minus Withholdings:	
Federal Income Taxes	$250
State Income Taxes	$110
City, State, or Local Income Taxes	
FICA	$30
401K	$84
Health Insurance	$86
Other Withholdings	$125
Net Income from Employment	**$1,765**
# of Pay Periods per Month	2
Net Income from Employment per Month	**$3,530**
Add Other ı Income:	
Interest	$24
Dividends	$12
Social Security	$9
Rent	$675
Gifts Received	$0
Total Other Income	$720
Total Net Income Available	**$4,250**

Unless you keep a scrupulous record of your expenditures, determining just where your money is going can take a bit of detective work. Pull out your checkbook, bank statements for the past few months, your credit card bills (to identify specific purchases and to record the debt service charge you pay as interest), utility bills, receipts, and anything else you have on hand that holds information about your expenses.

When you have your expense records before you, record them on the Cash Flow Analysis worksheet. After you have entered your net income and expenses, the worksheet will calculate the difference. That difference—whether positive or negative—is your cash flow.

In the Know

If you simply don't have enough information on hand about how you're spending your money, consider keeping an expense record for a month or two. Note everything—donations, unreimbursed business expenses, gas fill-ups, repairs, dry cleaning—to create a detailed profile of your cash flow.

Cash Flow Analysis

Net Monthly Income (from Net Income Analyzer) | $4,250

Less Monthly Expenses:

Housing

Rent or Mortgage	$1,450
Electric	$85
Heat	$110
Phone	$33
Internet Access	$33
Cable TV	$33
Water	$48
Other Utilities	$25
Real Estate Taxes	$275
Groceries	$275
Home Maintenance (from home maintenance and repair budget)	$125
Insurance	$112
	$2,604

Personal Care and Comfort

Clothing	$125
Laundry and Dry Cleaning	$80
Haircuts, Manicure, Massage, etc.	$30
Medical	$35
Dental	$25
Other	$0
	$295

Transportation

Auto Payments	$285
Public Transportation	$0
Gas	$150
Auto Maintenance and Repair	$25
Tolls and Other Commuting Costs	$0
	$460

Insurance

Health Insurance	$0
Life Insurance	$42
Disability Insurance	$0
Auto Insurance	$150
Other Insurance	$0
	$192

Entertainment

Dinners Out	$65
Liquor Store or Bar Tabs	$0
Concerts and Shows	$0
Vacations	$50
Gifts to Others	$25
Recreational Vehicle or Boat Costs	$0
	$140

Debt Service

Credit Cards	$350
Education Loans	$0
Other Loans	$0
	$350

Other

Unreimbursed Business Expenses	$0
Donations	$0
Children Costs	$0
Child Support or Alimony	$0
Education Expenses	$0
	$0

Miscellaneous Expenses

Misc 1	$0
Misc 2	$0
Misc 3	$0
	$0

Total Monthly Expenses | $4,041

Monthly Net Cash Flow | $209

If your cash flow is a positive number, congratulations! You're operating in the black and can selectively determine how to change your spending patterns to save even more money each month. If your cash flow is a negative number, you're spending more than you're making. That means you have to change your spending habits quickly and substantially, to avoid going further into the hole.

Budgeting Made Bearable

Whatever your cash flow situation might be, you need to create a budget you can live with—and then live with it. You've already done a lot of the heavy lifting, by setting your financial goals, determining your net worth, and calculating your cash flow. Now, you simply need to use that information to craft a plan for managing your income and outgoing expenses wisely. The Budgeting worksheet will help you in that process.

This worksheet builds upon the Cash Flow Analysis you've just completed, by adding columns for information about your budget and its effectiveness. Take a moment to consider every expense you recorded in your Cash Flow Analysis, then determine how much you believe you *should* (or can) afford to spend on that item.

After you've set your budgeting goals, you need to determine how well they work for you. Over the next month, record your *actual* expenses for each budgeted item. Where the budgeted and actual amounts vary, try to determine and record the reason for that variability. The information in this work-sheet gives you an in-depth look at your money management habits and capabilities.

Pitfall Alert!

Remember, you are setting the limits here, so don't feel resentful of this process. You are setting your own limits, for your own benefit. Budgeting isn't a financial straightjacket; it's your tool for getting more from the money you earn.

Managing Your Cash

Keeping tabs on utility bills, rent or mortgage payments, and so on is a relatively straight-forward process. Tracking down how you spend your pocket money can be much more difficult. You might drop $7.37 on a burger and fries at Ecoli to Go, then stop at the newsstand on the way back to the office and pay $5.13 for a *People Stalker* magazine, a candy bar, and some breath mints. On your way past your co-worker's desk, he reminds you that the Girls Stout cookies you ordered from his daughter are in (ouch, $12 for two dozen sugar cookies?). In one hour of your day, you've dropped nearly $25. And, oh no, here comes Janice with a birthday card for the boss and a gift-fund envelope to go with it. It's no wonder that money leaks out of your pocket faster than you may realize.

Budgeting

Net Monthly Income (from Net Income Analyzer)	$4,250	Budget	Actual	Variance	Explanation of Variance
Less Monthly Expenses:					
Housing					
Rent or Mortgage	$1,450	$1,450	$1,450	$0	
Electric	$85	$85	$65	$20	
Heat	$110	$115	$125	-$10	Extra cold month
Phone	$33	$33	$33	$0	
Internet Access	$33	$33	$33	$0	
Cable TV	$33	$33	$33	$0	
Water	$48	$48	$39	$9	Added water savers in all faucets and shower heads
Other Utilities	$25	$25	$17	$8	
Real Estate Taxes	$275	$275	$275	$0	
Groceries	$275	$225	$325	-$100	Spent extra for upcoming holiday dinner
Home Maintenance (from home maintenance and repair budget)	$125	$100	$75	$25	
Insurance	$112	$85	$68	$17	
	$2,604	$2,507	$2,538	-$31	
Personal Care and Comfort					
Clothing	$125	$125	$100	$25	
Laundry and Dry Cleaning	$80	$75.	$80	-$5	
Haircuts, Manicure, Massage, etc.	$30	$15	$20	-$5	
Medical	$35	$24	$16	$8	
Dental	$25	$15	$19	-$4	
Other	$0	$10	$7	$3	
	$295	$264	$242	$22	
Transportation					
Auto Payments	$285	$250	$150	$100	
Public Transportation	$0	$0	$15	-$15	
Gas	$150	$125	$180	-$55	
Auto Maintenance and Repair	$25	$30	$12	$18	
Tolls and Other Commuting Costs	$0	$15	$10	$5	
	$460	$420	$367	$53	
Insurance					
Health Insurance	$0	$12	$10	$2	
Life Insurance	$42	$120	$142	-$22	
Disability Insurance	$0	$12	$10	$2	
Auto Insurance	$150	$12	$16	-$4	
Other Insurance	$0	$1	$1	$0	
	$192	$157	$179	-$22	
Entertainment					
Dinners Out	$65	$50	$65	-$15	
Liquor Store or Bar Tabs	$0	$12	$8	$4	
Concerts and Shows	$0	$0	$0	$0	
Vacations	$50	$140	$74	$66	
Gifts to Others	$25	$15	$0	$15	
Recreational Vehicle or Boat Costs	$0	$0	$0	$0	
	$140	$217	$147	$70	
Debt Service					
Credit Cards	$350	$350	$385	-$35	
Education Loans	$0	$0	$0	$0	
Other Loans	$0	$0	$0	$0	
	$350	$350	$385	-$35	
Other					
Unreimbursed Business Expenses	$0	$0	$0	$0	
Donations	$0	$0	$0	$0	
Children Costs	$0	$0	$0	$0	
Child Support or Alimony	$0	$0	$0	$0	
Education Expenses	$0	$0	$0	$0	
	$0	$0	$0	$0	
Miscellaneous Expenses					
Misc 1	$0	$0	$0	$0	
Misc 2	$0	$0	$0	$0	
Misc 3	$0	$0	$0	$0	
	$0	$0	$0	$0	
Total Monthly Expenses	$4,041	$3,915	$3,858	$57	
Monthly Net Cash Flow	$209				

If you want to get serious about managing your money, you have to manage *all* of it. Budgeting a specific amount for your "miscellaneous" purposes is an essential step, but setting limits you can live with can be difficult.

If you're having trouble corralling your miscellaneous out-of-pocket expenses, the Cash Expense Journal is for you. Use it to record specific cash purchases you make every week.

Cash Expense Journal

Week of   /   /20

Item	Amount
Lunch out	$27.65
Dry Cleaners	$9.45
Tolls	$9.00
Newspaper	$4.75
Other:	
Random Act of Kindness - paid another person's toll on highway	$3.00
Prescription at pharmacy	$10.00
Bought flowers for administrative assistant	$25.00
Total Cash Expenses for Week	$88.85

All of the options for improving your cash flow fall within two categories—increasing your income or decreasing your expenses. Let's begin by clearing out the low-hanging fruit. Drop accounts (and monthly charges) for products or services you don't use (gym membership, premium cable channels, magazine subscriptions, and so on). Maybe you can sell some of your goods on eBay or in a garage sale, or do work you're currently hiring out (housecleaning, laundering, lawn maintenance). And, let's not forget cutting back on spending; get a grip on your inner consumer, and make it stop buying stuff you don't need. Or, you might be able to improve your income by taking on a part-time job or some freelance work or by putting together a good pitch for a raise or promotion (with a higher salary) at your current gig. Finally, make sure you're paying your lowest legal tax rate (see Chapter 8). Remember, you're in command of your cash flow, so make it work for you!

What If? Contingency Planning

Okay, you've built that budget and cleaned up your cash flow. Maybe you've even begun saving for next year's trip to Belize. Things are tight, but you know where you're going and how to get there. You are golden, my friend!

And then, everything blows up.

"Everything" meaning your furnace. No one was hurt, but you're looking at a couple of thousand dollars for a new system. And then gas prices double, which drives up the cost of food, cutting into your positive cash flow. And then, your husband falls down the basement steps (on his way to watch the furnace installation), and his insurance has a $2,000 deductible, so you know you'll be picking up a chunk of that tab, too. What can you do?

What you *can't* do is avoid unexpected expenses. So you have to have a contingency plan to help pay for them. Use the Contingency Funding worksheet to plan for the unplanned. Insurance deductibles and co-pays should take front-stage, since those are costs that you know might crop up during the year. If you have an ailing appliance, a car that's on elder-care, or another financial-hit-waiting-to-happen, record them on the worksheet, along with an estimate of the repair or replacement costs. Use the Explanation column as a reminder of how you arrived at your estimate. When you've completed the worksheet, go back to your budget and take a look at all of your expenses and income sources to determine—right now—how you could cover (or recover from) an unbudgeted financial hit.

Contingency Funding

Contingency	Amount	Explanation
Auto Insurance Deductible	$300.00	Save for 1 Incident
Home Insurance Deductible	$250.00	Save for 1 Incident
Medical or Dental Co-Pay	$50.00	Estimate Amount
Loss of Employment	$7,800.00	6 Months Living Expenses
Other Contingencies	$475.00	
Total Contingency Savings Desired	**$8,875.00**	

The Least You Need to Know

◆ Your cash flow is the difference between your net income and expenses.

◆ You can increase your cash flow by bringing in more money or reducing your expenses. Be open-minded in this process, and remember—increasing your cash flow will increase your financial security and lessen financial stress.

◆ A budget is your most powerful tool for managing your money.

◆ Keep a cash journal to learn where all of that "incidental" money is going, and to uncover wasteful spending habits you might want to kick.

◆ Make a contingency plan for dealing with unexpected financial blows—loss of income, major unplanned expenses, and so on. You may never need it, but it's better to plan for a crisis *before* it occurs.

Chapter 4

By the Book: Managing Your Financial Information

In This Chapter

- ◆ Having trauma-free money talks with family and other significant others
- ◆ Helping your parents make money plans
- ◆ Where it's at: organizing and storing financial information
- ◆ Choosing the documents you'll store

Lots of people have trouble talking about money, but that's no excuse for leaving your significant others in the dark about your family finances. Believe me, there is nothing blissful about remaining ignorant on the topic of how much money you and your spouse or life partner have, how much you owe, what investments you hold, and how far along you are in meeting your financial goals. If you have kids, they need to be some part of the family financial discussion—that's an important step in their education about money and its management. And you, your siblings, and parents need to be comfortable talking about family financial matters, too. The guidelines and worksheets in this chapter will help make "money talks" (including those with financial pros) relatively pain-free and incredibly productive.

This chapter isn't all talk, either. One of the most fundamental steps in building a strong financial plan is to organize and safely store your personal financial records. This chapter also offers worksheets to help you quickly determine what to store, where to store it, and how to make sure all of your documents are safely protected from intruders (even those of the cyber variety).

Sharing the Best-Kept Secrets

As much as you might like to think that you're "above all that" when it comes to money matters, you're not. Money is an integral part of your daily life, so you need to be comfortable talking about it. Married? You need to talk about money with your spouse. Children? Ditto—they have to learn how to manage money, too, you know. Even if you're committed to the free and single lifestyle, at some point you may need to step in and help your parents with their finances. In fact, you can almost count on it.

And family aside, money talk surrounds your personal and professional lives. If you want a raise, you need to be able to tell your boss why you deserve more money than you're currently making. If you hire a contractor to build an addition to your home, a plumber to install the shower, or an attorney to sue the contractor and the plumber for faulty work, you're going to have to talk money with each of them. Financial advisors, attorneys, real estate agents—as your savings and assets grow, so does the necessity for conferring about them with professionals.

Failure to have necessary financial discussions will add to your stress and subtract from your progress toward financial goals—which is not a good equation for personal financial freedom. Now is the time to get comfortable with the idea of talking about your finances. The worksheets and guidelines here will help you get started.

Making Finances a Family Affair

If you grew up in a family where a stiff-upper-lipped parent single-handedly managed the family finances and discouraged discussions about money, then it's time to put yet another family tradition out to pasture. Then, you can replace it with a new one: an ongoing (or, at least, annual) family conversation about money.

Don't view family discussions about money as an optional activity. Even if only one partner is a wage earner, even if nobody in the family wants to talk about money, even if—especially if—you're trying to recover from some embarrassing and stressful financial setbacks, everyone in your household has a stake and an influence in its financial management. Money management can be tough, but keeping everyone on the same financial page makes the task easier and the results more effective.

Now, I'm not recommending anything that involves a roped-off ring and announcer, or a PowerPoint presentation and whiteboard—although maybe your family would really enjoy some combination of all those. No, family money discussions need only cover a few essential topics. For a simple meeting between you and your spouse or partner, use the following list of essential topics. You can add specific items of concern in the space provided below each item:

Pitfall Alert!

Try not to lay ominous overtones on your family discussions of money matters. Instead, treat them as an opportunity to work together for something you all want—a better life with less financial strain and worry. Don't blame, criticize, or yell (and try not to take offense if others do).

◆ The current status of your finances (assets and debts; savings and investments)

_____

_____

_____

_____

◆ The effectiveness of your budget (Is it working? What problems does it present?)

_____

_____

_____

_____

◆ Your financial goals "progress report"

_____

_____

_____

_____

◆ The most important financial challenges you're facing (too much debt, loss of income, lack of savings, and so on)

_____

_____

_____

_____

 ◆ Financial management responsibilities (Is the current setup effective, or does it need revision?)

_____

_____

_____

_____

For family meetings that involve children, use the Family Discussion Topic List as a guide to prepare a "money talk" appropriate for your children's age groups. Next to each age-ranked topic, note specific concerns you want to cover during the discussion.

Family Discussion Topic List

Children under 18:   **Specific Concerns**
Basic financial education (earning, using, saving money)

Concept of delayed gratification

The difference between needs and wants

Budgeting exercises and practice

Children over 18:
Cost of living, education, and their role in controlling/taking on expenses

College payment plan

Career guidance

Children over 25:
Details of your estate plan

Each member's role in settling family estate

Location of important documents

Relationships with advisors
General awareness of your financial situation

Health, life, and long-term care insurance policy information

---

In the Know

> Do your children a favor and teach them about money management at an early age. You don't have to share all of your financial complications—no five-year-old should lie in bed at night worrying about how her parents will make their mortgage payment. On the other hand, it's only right that your child understand the concepts of earning, saving, and spending money at an early age. Give them an allowance, and help them set up their own budget. And remember: talking about money is the first step toward managing it—an important step for any child to take.

Talking Finances with Siblings and Elderly Parents

If you think talking with your spouse or partner about money is difficult, you might be even less anxious to have the conversation with your elderly parents. Many of us grew up with parents who would be more comfortable strolling on the beach in a Speedo than talking about their personal finances. Broaching the subject of money with your parents is a passage of sorts; you are officially declaring that you're no longer the "innocent" in need of protection, but are a full-fledged adult who can handle the facts of their financial life—and you want to be in a position to do that should the need arise. When the time is right, sit down with your parents and wade into the financial waters alongside them. The basics of that conversation should include:

- Their current financial condition—debts, assets, savings, and investments

- Their retirement plan and income

- The need for a *durable power of attorney*

- Where they keep their financial and legal records, insurance records, burial instructions, bank information, safe deposit numbers/key locations, and other important information

- Their health care wishes

def•i•ni•tion

A **durable power of attorney** document can assign you the legal authority to handle your parents' personal, financial, medical, and legal affairs. The "durable" in this term means that these rights continue on, even when the person assigning those rights becomes physically or mentally incapacitated.

The Parents/Sibling Discussion Checklist will help you consider topics that you may need to discuss with your parents about their finances—and the future. Check the item if your answer is "yes"; examine unchecked items to determine whether you need to discuss them in detail during your meeting.

If you have siblings, they should be involved in the talk, too. That may or may not make things easier, depending on your family dynamics (I leave those for you to sort through). But, you and your sibs need to have a plan in place for the care of your parents and their finances as they age. If one or both of them develops a need for full-time care or other assistance, you'll be glad you struggled through any difficulties in advance.

Parents/Sibling Discussion Checklist

☐ Do your parents have a durable power of attorney holder to act on their behalf in the event they are unable?

☐ Do you know who your parents' professional advisors are?

☐ Do your parents have wills, trusts, or other estate planning documents?

☐ If yes, are you aware of the provisions or asked to serve in any way?

☐ Do your parents have medical powers of attorney or health care proxies signed?

☐ If yes, is that document on file with their primary care physician?

☐ Do you know where your parents' important documents such as wills, trusts or insurance policies, deeds, auto titles, and financial statements are located?

☐ Do your parents own long-term care insurance?

☐ Do you have access to your parents' safety deposit box, if they have one?

☐ Do you have a key or other access to your parents' house?

☐ Do you have a list of and phone numbers for your parents' friends, neighbors, doctors, or other professional relationships?

Do your parents need help with:

☐ Bill paying

☐ Housekeeping

☐ Shopping

☐ Yard work

☐ Transportation

☐ Meals

☐ Grooming, dressing, or bathing

☐ Other: _____

Many parents find it easier to discuss their financial circumstances and arrangements with a professional. If your parents have a hard time having this conversation with you, offer to bring an estate planner or financial advisor into the mix. If you need to call in a pro, better to do it now than when you've landed in a family crisis.

Covering *All* Critical Money Conversations

Family members aren't the only folks you need to talk with about your financial affairs. Depending upon your financial plans and circumstances, there are a number of financial advisors and other professionals you may need to meet with to discuss specific aspects of your estate.

How to keep it all straight? The Financial Discussion Scheduler will help. Use the Professional Contacts and Personal Contacts lists to determine which people you might need to confer with about your financial situation. The Topics and Frequency lists outline the most important topics for each conversation and the frequency with which you should hold them. As you schedule your talks, note the date in the Scheduled Date column.

Financial Discussion Scheduler

To Whom	Topics	Frequency	Scheduled Date
Professional Contacts			
Tax Preparer	Taxes, tax planning, IRS notices, estimated payments	2x per year	
Attorney	Estate plan, business documents, real estate transactions, marriage and divorce, life-threatening illness	As needed	
Insurance Agent	Review coverage, develop risk and protection plan, gap analysis, renewal discussion	At least annually	
Benefits	Benefit review and renewal	At least annually	
Investment Advisor	Review asset allocation, risk tolerance, performance, objectives	At least annually	
Financial Planner	Financial check-up, life planning, strategy discussions, advice	At least annually	
Realtor	Buying or selling real estate	As needed	
Personal Contacts			
Spouse	Financial updates and plan progress, personal and financial objectives, lifestyle and family values	As needed	
Children	Success meter discussions, mutual expectations, financial education and leadership	Ongoing	
Parents	Estate and financial plan, contingency plan, lifestyle plan	As needed	
Siblings	Parent-related issues, their role in your estate plan and vice versa	As needed	
Executors	Notice of their role, duties and significance of role, letter of instruction, locations of important documents	As needed or changed	
Trustees	Clarification of role and duties, information about trust terms, alternate or co-trustees, time frame	As needed or changed	
Beneficiaries	Notification of beneficiary status, terms of beneficial interest, limitations on access, key provisions	As needed or changed	

Keeping Your Records Straight (and Safe)

Most of us don't need more information, we just need a more effective method for storing and using it. Whether you use a filing cabinet, a computer zip drive, or some combination of both, you need to know what records to keep, how long to keep them, and how to keep those records safe and accessible to those who need to use them.

What Documents Should You Store?

The first step in setting up your family financial records is determining exactly *what* information you need to store. The following table lists some guidelines for choosing what to lose and what to hang on to.

Record Retention Guidelines

Record	How Long to Keep It
Tax returns	7 years or forever if electronic storage is available
Bank statements	3 years
Cancelled checks	3 years
Personal health and medical records	Forever
Life insurance policies	While policy is in force plus 3 years after policy is no longer in force
Auto and home policies	Until new policy arrives or longer if any claims are in process
Pay stubs	Until W-2 arrives and agrees with last pay stub
Home repair invoices	Until house is sold
Warranty records Credit card statements	Until Warranty period is over 12 months for monthly statements and annual summaries for 3 years
Utility bills	3 months

Record	How Long to Keep It
Mortgage statements	Retain monthly statements for 12 months, annual statements for period of home ownership plus 3 years
Home closing and mortgage documents	Until home is sold plus 3 full tax years
Business formation documents	Until business is closed or sold plus 3 full tax years
Business purchase or sale documents	Until business is closed or sold plus 3 full tax years
Investment statements	Save monthly statements for 3 years and annual summaries until investments are sold plus 3 full tax years

Storing Important Records

Now that you know what records you're going to keep, you can determine the best way to keep them. You want to be able to access your important documents quickly, in case of an emergency. And you want the storage system to be logical, so it can be used by your spouse or partner, your accountant, or any other person who might have a (legal) reason for accessing your records.

Household records should be easily accessible for quick reference when paying bills, budgeting, or other ongoing financial tasks. Important records, on the other hand, should be stored with an eye toward safety first. Safe storage means fireproof, water-proof, and theft-proof. Use the Location of Important Documents worksheet to list the storage location of your most important financial and legal documents. (And remember to store the worksheet in a secure location, as well.)

> **? In the Know** _____
>
> The computer created the need for all of those passwords you use (to bank, pay bills, order online, and so much more), so why not let the computer help you keep track of them? Go online to learn more about password protection software such as Roboform (www.RoboForm.com), Password Safe (www.passwordsafe.com), or Key Wallet (www.keywallet.com) to secure and track your passwords.

Location of Important Documents

Document	Location
Wills, trusts, and other estate documents	
Financial records	
Tax returns	
Insurance policies	
Warranty records	
Auto titles	
Business documents	
Legal documents	
Deeds	
Major purchase records	
Master list of passwords	
List of professional advisors	
Other: _____	
Other: _____	
Other: _____	

The Least You Need to Know

♦ Frank discussions about money (with family, financial professionals, employers, contractors, and so on) are an important step toward controlling your money and your financial future.

♦ Have the "money talk" with your parents—before a crisis forces you and/or your siblings to play a role in managing their financial affairs.

♦ Your financial records need to be well-organized and accessible to you and anyone who shares (or might need to share) the management of your personal finances.

♦ Safety and security are your first considerations when developing a system for storing important documents and electronic passwords.

Part 2

Managing Expenditures

You have a lot of big decisions to make about how you're going to use your money. In Chapters 5 through 8, you get some practical advice and time-saving tools to help you make those decisions.

Planning to buy a home someday soon? We'll help you decide whether the time is right, and how to make sure that you're getting a home you can afford. You'll also learn how to save for other big-ticket purchases, such as cars, kids, vacations, and other facts of life.

Managing money also means managing debt, and this part carries some timely tools for keeping your relationship with credit solid and stress-free. And because financial planning involves protecting your assets, this part holds some valuable tools for that job. You can use the information and worksheets in this part to compare health and life insurance options, and to choose and track insurance for your home, car, and other valuable possessions. And we haven't forgotten one of the unavoidable hazards to your financial health—taxes!

Chapter 5

Planning for the Big Stuff: Major Expenditures

In This Chapter

- ◆ Considering the leap into home ownership
- ◆ Financing a major renovation
- ◆ Buying or leasing a car
- ◆ Saving for marriage, kids, vacations, and other expensive life events

You've seen how small expenses can leave a big dent in your bank account, and you've learned some smart tips for improving cash flow. But when it comes to funding the big expenditures in life—a home, a car, a wedding, a new baby, or a vacation to help forget about all of the money you spent on those other things—you need a solid plan. In this chapter, you get some tools to help with the hard work of planning for and financing major expenditures. From weighing the benefits of leasing versus buying a home or car, to funding a major home renovation, vacation, or other major expense, the worksheets in this chapter keep you on track and in charge of your financial destiny.

Is Home Ownership Right for You?

Every time that loud family in the next apartment starts haggling over who gets the last Pop Tart, you swear that you've had enough of the renter's life and are ready to buy your own home. Okay, that desire is understandable, but is buying a home a good move for you right now? If so, just how much home can you afford? The worksheets in this section of the chapter help you answer those questions.

Renting Versus Buying a Home

For years, real estate was considered one of the most secure investments you could make … until it wasn't. Today, most investment analysts agree that you should buy a home because you want to live in it, not because you want it to fund your retirement. So, if you can't count on your home's value doubling as soon as you sign the paperwork, are there any *real* benefits to owning versus renting a home? Yes, there are. At the same time, renting offers its own set of advantages, too.

? In the Know

If you're relocating to a new city, consider renting for a short while after the move. No matter how good your real estate agent might be, it's always wise to get to know the area before making a commitment about where you'll invest in a home.

Weighing the pros and cons of ownership versus renting? The following table offers a snapshot of the "alternative realities" of both arrangements. Which benefits have the most appeal for you?

Finding Your Identity: Renter or Homeowner?

Benefits of Renting	Benefits of Home Ownership
You can move as often as you like (and your lease allows).	You can settle in and become part of the neighborhood.
You don't have to hassle with home maintenance.	You can fix your place any way you want to.
You aren't cluttering up your debt load with a mortgage.	You want your monthly payments to build equity for *you*, not a landlord.

Benefits of Renting	Benefits of Home Ownership
You don't have to come up with a down payment and other upfront costs.	You want the fixed monthly payments and tax breaks of ownership.

But aside from the emotional reasons for home ownership, you need to consider the practical financial pros and cons. The Rent Versus Home Ownership Comparison worksheet can help you form an *approximate* idea of how the upfront and monthly costs of renting versus owning a home compare. Again, these figures will vary with your home or apartment's size, condition, and—of course—location, location, location.

No matter where or what type of home you buy, you have some upfront costs to consider:

- ◆ **The down payment:** The days of "no down payment" mortgages are gone. Count on coming up with at least 10, and more likely 20 percent or more of the home's purchase price as a down payment. If you pay less than 20 percent down, you're likely to have to carry *private mortgage insurance*, or PMI.

def•i•ni•tion

Private Mortgage Insurance (or PMI) is a monthly cost you'll bear when you put down less than 20 percent as a down payment toward a mortgage. It protects your lender if you default on the loan. PMI rates vary, according to the amount of your down payment and the type of loan you've secured. For current rates, visit www.pmi-us.com/rates.

- ◆ **Inspection fees:** You'll need to have the home inspected for structural integrity, termites, asbestos, and so on. These costs vary; check with your real estate agent for an estimate.

- ◆ **Closing costs:** Your mortgage company will tack on all sorts of fees, for surveys, property taxes, title insurance, and so on. Costs vary, but you can estimate them at about 5 percent of the price you pay for the home.

- ◆ **Points:** Some mortgage lenders charge points—a lump sum amount of interest up front—which can lower the loan's interest rate. Each point is 1 percent of the total loan amount.

These loan-associated costs aren't your only up-front expenses of home ownership. You might also have to do some essential fix-ups, like rewiring a home office or repainting, and you might need to pick up some new furnishings (what—you didn't have a billiard room in your old apartment?).

What about the ongoing costs of renting versus owning a home?

- **Insurance:** Homeowner's and renter's insurance rates vary dramatically, depending upon the location and value of the property being insured. You can go online to compare quotes for your area at sites such as www.compuquotes.com. The Insurance Information Institute also provides national averages. (For more information on these types of insurance policies, see Chapter 7).

- **Property taxes:** Homeowners pay property taxes, which nationally average about 1.5 percent of total property value annually. For a $300,000 property, therefore, you could estimate these taxes at about $375 a month. Your county auditor's office can tell you local rates.

- **Repairs and maintenance:** No crystal ball can predict the costs of maintaining a home, but most sources say to estimate that you'll spend about 2 percent of a home's value on repairs and maintenance every year. Divide that amount by 12 to estimate your monthly costs.

In the Know

Homeowners get tax breaks for the amount of loan interest and property tax they pay. You also might qualify for home office deductions. You learn more about specific tax issues in Chapter 8, but for now, just realize that home ownership might *reduce*, rather than add to, your tax burden.

- **Rental inflation:** If you buy a home with a fixed interest rate (one in which the rate never changes), your mortgage payments will never go up. Renters, however, can expect rental charges to go up every year. Many landlords adjust rents to match the rate of inflation; others use their own system ("Hey, I need a new car this year, so I gotta charge you more for your apartment"). You can estimate that your rent will generally increase by the annual inflation rate, adjusted by supply and demand factors in your local market. For purposes of this analysis, start with 4 to 5 percent a year and then adjust it to reflect your local market.

With your research results in hand, use the Rent Versus Home Ownership Comparison worksheet to calculate the up-front and ongoing costs of home ownership, and to compare those costs to those of renting.

Rent Versus Home Ownership Comparison

Rental Costs:

Monthly Rent Cost	$1,100
Monthly Utilities	$425
Insurance - monthly payment	$48
Other (essential fix-ups, furnishings, etc.)	$575
Total Monthly Costs of Renting	**$2,148**

Home Ownership Costs:

Monthly Mortgage Payment	$1,056
Interest Rate of Mortgage	5.00%
Length of Mortgage - in years	20
Property Taxes	$250
PMI	$0
Insurance - monthly payment	$175
Utilities	$425
Maintenance/Repairs	$333
Homeowner Association Fees	$175
Other	$100
Total Monthly Cost of Owning	**$2,514**

Monthly Cost Difference Between Renting and Owning	**$366**

Upfront Costs of Ownership:

House Purchase Price	$200,000
Down Payment (assumes 20% down payment)	$40,000
Closing Costs	$2,000
Mortgage Points	$4,000
Other (essential fix-ups, furnishings, etc.)	$2,500
Total Upfront Costs of Ownership	**$48,500**

How Much Home Can You Afford?

When you've made the decision to become a homeowner, you have to immediately make another important decision: you absolutely will not buy a house you cannot afford to furnish or maintain (without living on ramen noodles and ketchup). For some reason, the bigger the commitment, the more our emotions struggle to take the wheel of the decision-making process. Fight that urge! You won't be able to enjoy a house you can't afford to keep.

Remember, the mortgage payment is only the tip of the monthly debt iceberg. In addition to taxes, insurance, utilities, and maintenance, remember to consider essential new furnishings, neighborhood association fees, and so on. Even the driving distance to your work, the grocery, and other frequent destinations play a role in how much it costs for you to live where you live.

Fortunately, you don't have to go it alone (or rely on the advice of an eager real estate agent) when determining whether that home you're considering fits into your financial future. Most financial advisors recommend that you spend no more than 28 percent of your total income for housing, and no more than 40 percent of your total income on all debt (including car loans, student loans, credit cards, and so on). You already estimated the total ongoing monthly costs of home ownership in the previous Rent Versus Home Ownership Comparison worksheet. Collect that information, along with the monthly figures for other debts you're carrying, and plug the amounts into the Home Affordability Engine worksheet (the Budgeting worksheet you completed in Chapter 3 contains your debt information). The Home Affordability Engine worksheet will calculate your total monthly costs of ownership and your total monthly debt load and calculate those costs as percentages of your income, to determine whether that home you're considering fits in your financial fitness plan.

Renovating Your Home

Signing the dotted line on the mortgage papers—and there are a bunch of them, believe me—rarely means that you're finished making big financial commitments to your homestead. At some point you may find yourself facing a major home makeover project. Whether you're redoing the kitchen, adding a guest bathroom, or building a new deck for outdoor parties, renovations can mean big money. And, as you have heard me say so often in this book, that requires a financial plan!

Pitfall Alert!

Reliable and competent contractors may seem to be as rare and elusive as Sasquatch or the Loch Ness Monster. Don't be lulled into trusting a contractor just because he shows up (as unusual as this might be). Ask for and check references, and look to local service screeners, such as Angie's List (www.angieslist.com), to check the costs and quality of any contractor you're considering.

Home Affordability Engine

Monthly Mortgage Payment	$900
Monthly Property Tax Bill	$300
Monthly Insurance Premiums	$100
Total Monthly Principal, Interest, Taxes, and Insurance Costs (PITI)	**$1,300**
Gross Annual Household Income	$75,000
Gross Monthly Household Income	$6,250
Principal, Interest, Taxes, and Insurance Costs as a Percentage of Monthly Household Income	**21%**
Other Monthly Debt and Loan Payments	
Auto Loans	$300
Education Loans	$100
Credit Cards	$150
Personal Loans	$25
Other Debt Service	$0
Total Other Monthly Debt and Loan Payments	**$575**
Total PITI and Other Monthly Debt and Loan Payments	**$1,875**
Divide Total Other and Housing by Gross Monthly Income	**30%**

To qualify for a mortgage, your principal, interest, taxes, and insurance (PITI) should be less than 28% of gross household income, and PITI plus other monthly debt and loan payments should be less than 40% of gross household income.

To construct such a plan, you'll need to consider a few factors:

♦ **Estimated cost of purchase:** Shopping around for prices on a new major appliance, carpeting, or other renovation-related purchase is a relatively easy exercise. Go online or hit the stores! But for labor costs (painting, construction, wiring, and so on), you'll have to get contractor estimates.

♦ **The return rate on your savings vehicle:** If you're stashing money in a CD or other interest-bearing plan, remember to account for the return on that investment.

♦ **Your target date:** How long do you have to save the money? The length will determine what kind of savings plan you use and how much interest that plan will accrue.

When you've done your homework, use the Major Purchases Schedule to determine how much you'll need to save every month in order to hit the goal of having enough money to pay for your renovation by your chosen date. Can't afford to set aside that much money every month? In that case, consider:

- Scaling back the extent of the renovation

- Doing some of the work yourself

- Extending your deadline

- Cutting back on other expenses so you can stash more away for the renovation (see Chapter 3 for more information about budgeting)

Major Purchases Schedule

Item	Cost	Desired Date of Acquisition	Number of Months Until Acquisition	Monthly Savings Plan to Reach Goal
Family room renovation				
Carpet replacement				
Light fixtures				
Repainting walls				
New sofa				
50" plasma TV				

On the Road: Buying or Leasing a Car

Most Americans own a car, whether or not they need one. And all of those commuter-polluters have, at some point, found themselves locked in a soul-killing experience from which they think they'll never escape. No, I'm not talking about a rush-hour traffic jam. I'm talking about an automobile dealership.

Whether you lease or buy your car, you *will* have to deal with a dealer. And you can almost count on the fact that that person won't be completely up front with you about all of the negative repercussions of your decision. So allow me to do just that.

Buying a car is a good idea if you plan to hang on to the thing until it disintegrates—and, I should add, when you're committed to a maintenance plan that will increase the chances that the disintegration occurs long after you've made your final payment. And remember, cars depreciate quickly, so you can't consider your automobile an investment.

Leasing a car can be a good idea when you plan to switch vehicles every few years, and if you need (that's right, *need*) a vehicle that's a bit more than you could afford to buy outright. You probably won't need a down payment to lease a car, and you can give it back to the dealership when your lease ends. A closed-end lease lets you simply return your car at the end of the lease period and wave as you exit the dealership. An open-end lease might require you to pay the difference between the car's current market value and the value the dealer assigned to it when you signed your lease (called the residual value). Lease payments are usually less than auto loan payments for the same vehicle, because when you lease, you're really only paying for the car's depreciation. On the other hand, total costs for leasing are almost always higher than the cost of buying the same car. Your lease agreement is likely to have mileage limits, and you're still on the hook for maintenance costs. In the end, leasing a vehicle is often more expensive than buying one.

Automobile leases tend to be e-x-t-r-e-m-e-l-y complicated, and terms vary wildly among geographic regions and dealerships. You can gather lease details from local auto dealerships, or go online for more information (www.leaseguide.com and www. federalreserve.gov both offer great guides to auto leases).

If you're still on the fence, you need a more detailed analysis to determine whether to lease or buy your ride. To compare rates and calculate costs, gather some basic information from at least three dealerships:

- Monthly payment estimates and term-length for both loan and lease agreements

- The value of any trade-ins, rebates, or dealer discounts applicable to your deal

- Sales tax associated with both purchase and lease agreements

- Title and registration fees

- Residual purchase price for leased vehicle; the dealership determines this value, which represents the price of the vehicle at the end of its lease

With this information in hand, you can calculate the true costs of your purchase or lease agreement. Use the Auto Lease Versus Purchase Comparison worksheet to make this comparison for any dealership's offer.

Auto Lease Versus Purchase Comparison

Leasing Costs

Vehicle Selling Price	$	17,500
Sales Tax	$	875
Title and Registration	$	450
Other Costs	$	68
Less Down Payment and/or Trade-In	$	1,500
Cash Down at Purchase	$	750
Net Purchase Price	$	16,643
Monthly Lease Payment		**$390.86**

Purchase Costs

Vehicle Selling Price	$	17,500
Sales Tax	$	875
Title and Registration	$	450
Other Costs	$	68
Less Down Payment and/or Trade-In	$	1,500
Cash Down at Purchase	$	1,500
Net Purchase Price	$	15,893
Monthly Car Ownership Payment		**$373.25**
Net Monthly Savings with Lease		(**$17.61**)

Marriage, Kids, Vacations, and Other Life Events

After you get married, the big-ticket items you need to plan for can multiply exponentially. The wedding itself, for example, can be a real financial ball and chain if you don't plan carefully (and if you don't have a happy parent showering you with loads of no-strings-attached money to make it happen). Then there's the honeymoon, and that new washer and dryer, and maybe a new home in which to do your laundry.

And, if all goes well, you might have a baby or two. The plus sign shimmering to the surface of a pregnancy testing wand shouldn't be your signal to *start* saving for a family. If you want to be able to focus on the other demands of pregnancy and new parenthood, you need to have some savings set aside to cover the start-up costs, such as health care deductibles, lost work time, clothes and furnishings, and childcare. After that, you have a mere 18 years or so of support, clothing, school costs, wear and tear on the refrigerator, and so on. Then, there's the major hit of paying for a college education. And then, before you know it, it's time for another wedding. And this time, whether or not you're footing the bill, *you* don't get to go on the honeymoon.

In the Know

If you're starting a family, now is the time to think about how (and whether) you'll help pay for your child's college education. According to www.collegeboard.com, in 2008–2009, college costs (tuition, room/board, and fees) averaged just over $35,000 a year for private four-year schools and more than $17,000 annually for public four-year schools. That rate goes up about 7 percent a year, too. Of course, over half of most students receive some sort of grant or financial aid. You don't have to count on the kindness of strangers, though. You can start saving right away for your child's college costs. Ask a financial advisor, or go online to find information about college savings plans such as the Coverdell Education Savings Accounts or 529 Prepaid Tuition or Savings Plans. These offer some tax breaks and they give your child a solid boost in the climb up those ivy towers.

Don't get me wrong—family isn't the *only* source of costly blips in our life passage. You might decide that you absolutely have to have that Sharkmaster boat you saw in the showroom last summer. Maybe you really want to get your teeth capped—whatever it costs! Maybe you wake up one morning and decide that making goat cheese is your true calling in life, and you need to save a chunk of money to buy some goats (and a book on how to make goat cheese). In any event, saving up makes any life event easier and more enjoyable (or, at least, more bearable). With savings in hand you have more control over the event, and you don't have to engorge your debt burden to fund your dreams (or life's demands).

Where you stash your savings—certificates of deposit, mutual funds, passbook savings, that mayonnaise jar under your bed—will determine how much interest your savings will gather. The speed of your need (are you saving to replace a car that's about to collapse, or are you saving for your 10-month-old's college education?) will play a role in determining what kind of savings plan is right for you (see Chapter 9 for tools to help with savings and investment basics).

Thinking about saving up for a big event? Let's take this in two stages. First, use the Life Event Savings Planner to lay out the basics: what event you want to save for, how much you estimate you'll need to save, and how long you have to save it.

The Life Event Savings Planner gives you a good overview of the types of expenses you know are waiting for you down the road. Now, it's time to get serious. Use the Target Savings Guide to determine how much you'll need to save every month in order to hit each of your "big event" savings goals. You can discuss savings plans and account types with an agent at your bank or with a financial advisor, to determine which savings vehicle has the term limits and interest rates that work best for you.

Life Event Savings Planner

Life Event	Anticipated Date	Anticipated Cost	Months to Save
Wedding	May-12	$100,000	24
Parents' 25th Anniversary Gift	Nov-11	$1,500	17
Trip for 10th College Reunion	Jun-13	$3,000	37
Childbirth			
Bar Mitzvah			
Purchase of Second Home			

Pitfall Alert! _____

When you're setting your savings goals, don't forget that you'll need to add a bit of padding to your goal, to account for taxable interest and inflation. Tax rates vary, as does the rate of inflation, but in general, add about 10 percent of the total for every year you'll be saving toward your goal.

When you're ready to get serious about saving for a big event, turn to the Target Savings Guide. In the Targeted Savings Amount line, enter the amount of money you estimate that you'll need for your life event. Next, enter the number of months you have until your event date and the interest rate offered by your savings vehicle. The electronic version of the worksheet will calculate the amount of money you must save every month to meet your goal.

Target Savings Guide

Targeted Savings Amount in Today's Dollars	$	30,000
Number of Years Until Savings Is Needed		6
Annual Inflation		4.0%
Inflated Targeted Savings Amount	$	37,960
Months to Save		72
Earnings on Savings *		6%
Monthly Savings		$439

* Assumes an after-tax rate of return

The Least You Need to Know

♦ Sometimes renting is better than owning your home. Instead of buying into the "American Dream" mythology, decide on home ownership based on your needs, lifestyle, and financial situation.

♦ Major renovations require careful financial planning (and a contractor who has passed a detailed selection process).

♦ Buying a car may be a better choice than leasing one—or not. In either case, consider your finances, motivations, and needs (not your ego) when determining how much you want to invest in an automobile.

♦ Any big life event can require big spending. Plan ahead and save ahead to give yourself more control over how much you can spend.

6

Borrowing, Credit, and Debt Leverage

In This Chapter

- ◆ How to fight ugly debt buildup
- ◆ Making debt work for you
- ◆ Looking your best for lenders
- ◆ Dealing with debtors
- ◆ Coming to terms with your credit issues

Remember the "gilded age" of credit? You know, back when loans were available with a wink and a handshake and credit card offers flooded your mailbox every day, many of them addressed to your dog? Well, those days are no more, although many of us still feel the hangover. Still, credit will always be at the center of our personal (and national) economy, so you need to know how to manage debt wisely.

This chapter offers a number of tools for getting a handle on your personal debt and making it work for you. From organizing your credit cards to calculating the true costs of a loan and cleaning up your credit report, the worksheets in this chapter are ready to help you wrestle your debt load into submission. And, if your past … ahem … credit indiscretions have come back to haunt you, this chapter offers some useful tools for dealing with collection agencies and debt counselors. In other words, this chapter will help you control debt before it controls *you*.

Managing Debt

Credit is the engine that keeps our economy moving. Until it seizes up, that is. Anyone who thinks they don't need to manage their use of debt hasn't watched television, read a newspaper, or tried to take out a loan in the past few years. In short, our relationship with credit is on the skids. We often borrow too much, spend too much, and ignore reality. Credit can do that to you, but it doesn't have to.

Borrowing is a fact of life for most adults. Few of us are going to haul a satchel of cash into the automobile dealership or real estate closing meeting, and say, "Just give me my change and a receipt." We *need* credit for lots of things, and there's nothing wrong with using it. But we have to make our use of credit work *for* our long-term financial health—not against it.

The worksheets in this section of the chapter help you get on top and stay on top of your debt load. Use them to sort through and manage your credit cards, record secured debts, calculate the true cost of home mortgages and other loans, and to make sure you get any available tax advantages resulting from your debt load.

Your total debt load matters, for reasons you'll read about throughout this chapter—and this book, for that matter. If you're paying out more than 35 to 40 percent of your monthly gross income toward debt, you have a debt problem. Use the tools in this chapter to confront your debt situation and, if necessary, improve it.

Getting a Handle on Credit Card Debt

Debt comes in two forms—*secured* and *unsecured*. Secured debt is debt for which you've offered up some sort of collateral. If you take out a home equity loan, your … yes, you've guessed it … home becomes your collateral. Most credit cards, on the other hand, are unsecured. The sometimes lavish interest charges on these cards more than make up for the temporary loans the companies extend to cardholders. Secured debt tends to carry lower interest rates and fees than does unsecured debt.

def•i•ni•tion

Secured debt is debt for which you've offered up some form of collateral, such as a car, a home, or other secure holding. If you fail to repay a secured debt, the lender can take ownership of the property you've offered as collateral. **Unsecured debt** is that for which you have offered no collateral. If you fail to pay off unsecured debt, the lender can sue you or garnish your wages (and will hound you mercilessly until you pay up).

Some companies offer secured credit cards, which are, in effect, simply credit cards issued by the Bank of YOU. You deposit a set amount—$500 or $1,000, for example—with the credit card company. Then, you can use the card to charge up to the amount of your deposit. You can make payments to "top up" your balance, or the company may even float you a few hundred dollars in exchange for your good payment history. Folks who don't have established credit or who have hit a few bumps on the credit trail can use secured cards to reserve hotel rooms, rent a car, or other exchanges that almost always requires the use of a credit card.

We all like to think that we have a handle on our use of credit, but in reality, many of us have flown off that handle long ago. Are you one of them? Ask yourself the following questions:

◆ Do you use your credit card to "extend" your income?

◆ Have you made more than one late payment on a credit card in the past year?

◆ Do you pay only the minimum payment on any of your credit cards?

◆ Do you ever fail to check the purchases listed on the monthly statements or ignore the total balance on one or more of your credit cards?

If you answered Yes on *any* of these questions, you need to change your credit habits right away. As countless sources have suggested, you might be wise to cut up your cards or at least lock them away until you've paid off the balance. Using credit cards to pay for things your income won't cover is never the answer. If you can't afford it, don't buy it. That sounds harsh, but the simple fact is that we all have to live within our financial boundaries. If you make late payments, you'll pay a whopping late fee (over $30) and the company might increase your interest rate to 30 percent, 40 percent, or more. Racking up a huge balance and dabbing away at it with minimum payments is akin to piling your money in the driveway and setting it on fire. You'll be paying for the stuff you bought long after you've broken, lost, or grown tired of it. And ignoring your statement is never the answer for debt anxiety, but it might allow a thief to take his own sweet time in charging up purchases on your account.

The best way to understand your credit situation is to stare it in the face. Use the Credit-Watch Calculator to lay out the facts of your credit card collection—and debt. Enter each credit card's name, account number, outstanding balance, interest rate, and typical monthly payment amount. If you're carrying debt on multiple cards, some with high interest rates, this organizer gives you an opportunity to consider paying off and canceling some of those cards, moving debt to a card with a lower interest rate, or otherwise cleaning up your credit card act.

Credit-Watch Calculator

Credit Card Issuer	Account Number	Account Balance	Interest Rate	Monthly Payment
MasterMoney	5555-555-5555	$1,250	19%	$50
ExpressCash	11-1111-1111	$3,750	16%	$150

Totals

If you own your own small business, you've probably had multiple offers for business credit cards. These cards can serve a great purpose, by enabling you to cover up-front expenses that you'll recover later from clients, before the card's payment due date (many business cards require full payment every month). But what happens if your client defaults? Yes, you can go after the client in court, but that won't make that OVERDUE NOTICE from your credit card company go away any time soon. Depending upon the structure of your business and your agreement with the credit card company, your personal credit could be fouled up for seven years if your business card debt runs into problems. If your business demands that you have this kind of credit card, be prepared to call upon a backup plan to cover client defaults. See if you can negotiate a partial payment schedule with the business card company, or consider transferring the charge to a card that allows you to make partial payments. Then, do whatever you can to pay off that debt quickly, to avoid bleeding your financial fountain dry with excessive interest charges.

Pitfall Alert!

The more credit cards you carry, the more likely you are to use (and abuse) them. Credit cards are useful for establishing a good credit record, but they can just as quickly destroy one. I recommend that you keep your credit cards to a minimum; one, maybe two, general credit cards should give you ample emergency cash access. Beyond that, you're asking for trouble.

Tracking Secured Debts

Credit cards may not be the only debt load you're carrying right now. You might also have a home equity loan, automobile loan, or other secured debt. You need to keep track of those loans, of course, but you also need to consider them as part of your total debt load, in order to form a full and clear understanding of how you're using credit, and how much you're paying for the privilege. Use the Schedule of Secured Debt to list and track all of your secured debt agreements, the collateral you've used to secure each loan, the total amount of money you've borrowed, the interest rates, and the amounts of your monthly payments. How does your debt compare to your income? If you're spending more than you're making, you have a debt disaster brewing.

Schedule of Secured Debt

Debt Description	Security Pledged	Loan Amount	Interest Rate	Monthly Payment
Home Equity Loan	Home Equity	$20,000	8.50%	$120.00
Auto Loan	Auto	$17,000	6.50%	$403.15

Total Monthly Debt Payments	$ 523.15
Net Income	$ 4,200.00
Monthly Debt Payments as a Percentage of Income	12%

In the Know _____

The lower the cost of the debt, the less "ugly" that debt becomes. Student loans and many mortgages are just two examples of debt that carries a low interest rate, and therefore low cost. You need to consider how your total debt burden compares to your total annual income, of course, but getting rid of high interest rate debt should be your first concern.

Home Mortgages and Lines of Credit

I talked about home mortgages in Chapter 5, so I won't go through all of the details of holding one here. Also, I won't repeat all of the information about the associated costs of taking out a mortgage—there are plenty of them, so you might want to go back to Chapter 5 for a refresher. But if you're contemplating buying a home, one of the most important things you'll need to determine is what kind of monthly mortgage payment you can afford to make.

The Loan Calculator worksheet is a simple tool for determining the monthly payments for a mortgage (or any other loan), based on the amount of the loan, the length of the mortgage, and the interest rate. Plug in those values to calculate your monthly payment for any loan.

Loan Calculator

Amount Borrowed	$ 25,000
Payback Time Period (Length of Loan in Years)	4
Interest Rate	6%
Monthly Payment	$587

Interest rates go up and down all the time, and they can significantly change the total cost of a loan. For years, the common wisdom told us that you should only refinance if interest rates drop by 2 points or more, but that advice isn't necessarily sound. In addition to lower interest rates, you have to consider a number of other questions when making the decision to refinance:

◆ Is lowering your current monthly payment the most important issue for you right now? If interest rates have dropped even by one point, and you keep the same (or longer) repayment schedule, your monthly payments will be noticeably lower.

◆ How much will this refinancing cost you? Even if you don't have to pay a loan origination fee or points (a big "if"), closing costs for a six-figure loan may be anywhere from $800 to $2,000, depending on your lender.

◆ How long do you intend to stay in the home? If you're planning to move next year, you may not recover the costs of refinancing. If you're going to be in your home for another three to five years, however, you probably will come out ahead. And the longer you stay in the home, the greater your savings will be.

You probably could use some help in sorting through these weighty issues. If so, use the Refinance Benefit/Cost Calculator worksheet to calculate just how you'll come out on any refinancing deal you're mulling over.

When you're considering refinancing a mortgage, grab the details of your current loan (the remaining balance, the number of months left to pay on the loan, interest rate, and amount of monthly payments) along with the new loan amount, interest rate, and monthly payment. The worksheet will calculate the total amount of interest you'll pay for both loans.

Refinance Benefit / Cost Calculator

Balance Left on Loan	$110,000
Months Left on Current Loan	276
Interest Rate on Current Loan	6.50%
Monthly Payment on Current Loan	$769
Total interest to be paid on remainder of Loan Term	$102,236
New Loan Amount	$115,000
Length of New Loan (**months**)	360
New Mortgage Interest Rate	5.75%
New Mortgage Monthly Payment	$671
Total Interest to be Paid on New Mortgage	$126,599
Difference in Total Interest Payments	-$24,363

Closing Costs for New Loan

Points	$2,500
Appraisals	$400
Legal	$300
Inspections	$300
Credit Check	$200
Title	$300
Application fee	$75
Other	$125
Other	$0
Other	$0
Total Closing Costs for New Loan	$4,200
Monthly Payment Savings	$98
Time Period to Break Even From New Loan	43

In the Know _____

When weighing the costs of refinancing, don't forget to take into consideration the tax breaks you receive for interest payments. If you lower the amount of interest you're paying, you'll also lower the amount of that deduction.

Chances are, you'll pay less interest over the life of your new loan—after all, that's the major benefit of refinancing. But you still haven't calculated the actual benefit of the new loan. To do that, you need to subtract the costs of the loan process. Use the Closing Costs for New Loan section of the worksheet to record all of the costs associated with your new loan. The worksheet will calculate your total costs, then calculate how many months it will take for the new venture to break even (when you'll have saved enough in lowered interest payments to offset the costs of the refinancing).

Maintaining Your Credit Report

We have no secrets when it comes to our credit history. From the moment that you signed up for your first GAP credit card, you've been writing the story of your relationship with debt—and it's a story that every other creditor you've dealt with has read and contributed to. Remember that time you joined the InForLife music club, and triggered $800 in debt—while you were still in high school? And who could forget that time you let the bills stack up while you were hiking around Europe for four months? Well, your creditors certainly won't forget. And if they do, your credit report will remind them. The report includes a complete record of your past credit transactions—credit cards, mortgages, car loans, and so on—including whether you missed payments. Although these histories typically don't include rent and utility payments, _any_ payment that you've let go more than 90 days overdue could come back to haunt you through this report.

How does your credit report look? You can find out (free of charge once a year), by contacting any of the "big three" credit reporting agencies:

♦ **Experian:** www.experian.com or 1-888-397-3742

♦ **Equifax:** www.equifax.com or 1-800-685-1111

♦ **TransUnion LLC:** www.transunion.com or 1-877-322-8228

As you borrow and repay money, you're also racking up a credit score. This score is assigned by FICO (Fair Isaac Corporation), and it is simply a number that "grades" your credit history. The scores range between 300 and 850, with most people scoring in the 600–700 part of that range. High scores equal great credit history; low scores, not so much. Lenders determine whether or not to lend you money and how much to charge you for the loan based on your FICO score. If a 750 score lands you a 5.5 percent interest rate, a 580 might ratchet the interest rate on the same loan up to 8.5 percent. The score matters, in other words.

You need to check your credit history and score at least once a year, to determine how you're looking to potential lenders. If you're planning to buy a home, car, or other major purchase, it's a good idea to see what potential lenders will see when they check your credit status. The review will also reveal any inaccuracies on your history or identity theft shenanigans that have dinged your credit unfairly. If you uncover discrepancies (What?? I didn't buy the Chrysler Building!), you can contact the reporting agency and ask for corrections. You can also add your own comments to explain your side of any past problems.

Your credit report is a "living" document. You can fix it if it goes bad. If you want to buff up your credit history and score to woo a potential lender, start at least a year in advance of your loan application—longer is better. Use the Credit Improvement Checklist to work your way through a credit report makeover. Check those items that you are doing now or are committed to doing. Then, every month, revisit the list to determine that you're still on-track, and to ask yourself if you're ready to take on any of the unchecked items. Go on—rewrite history!

Pitfall Alert! _____

Don't make a weekly habit of checking your credit score or reports, and don't apply for too many credit cards at once. A blizzard of requests for your credit report can actually reduce your credit score. By law, credit reporting agencies must give you one free report a year. Beyond that, you may have to pay for reports you (not a creditor) have requested.

In addition to all of the previously-listed steps, you can commit to a plan for reducing your debt. The Debt Reduction worksheet will get you started on that path. List your debts, their balance and interest rates, and minimum monthly payment amounts. In the last column of the worksheet, assign a targeted payoff date for each debt. Then, every month, commit to making an additional payment on some or all of the accounts. When you do, record the payment on the worksheet.

Credit Improvement Checklist

☐   Review your credit report.

☐   Fix errors on your credit report.

☐   Have credit cards, but only a few.

☐   Pay your bills on time.

☐   Get current and stay current.

☐   If you anticipate having trouble staying current, contact the creditor to try to negotiate alternate payment arrangements.

☐   Keep balances low on credit cards.

☐   Don't open new credit card accounts that you don't need, even if it means another 10% off on a small purchase or a free T-shirt.

☐   Don't open a lot of new accounts in succession.

☐   Don't review your credit report too frequently. Many checks to your credit report for new debt will lower your credit rating.

☐   Don't bounce checks.

☐   Avoid letting accounts get turned over to a collection agency.

☐   Don't change jobs too often.

☐   Don't change residences too often.

☐   Stop using your credit cards.

Debt Reduction

	Balance	Interest Rate	Minimum Monthly Payment	Additional Monthly Payment	Targeted Payoff Date
Debt 1					
Debt 2					
Debt 3					
Debt 4					
Debt 5					
Debt 6					
Debt 7					
Total	$_____		$_____	$_____	

Collection Agencies, Credit Counseling, and Debt Consolidation

Okay, you hope it never comes to this, but sometimes debt can take control of your life. If you've let bills stack up for more than a month or two, you're likely to start receiving a lot of not-so-friendly calls from creditors and collection agencies. Even though these folks are regulated by the Federal Trade Commission (FTC), they may hound you mercilessly, even calling or dropping in at your place of business (you can ask your creditors in writing to leave you alone at work, and the law says they have to honor your request).

The best way to avoid this humiliation is to strike first. If you know that you won't be able to make full payments on any of your debts, contact the lenders or creditors immediately and ask to work out an alternative payment plan. Believe me, no department store or credit card company wants to hire a collection agency to hound you for money. They'd much rather you'd work with them to resolve your debt difficulties.

In the Know

If you think your creditors are treating you unfairly, take a stand. The government offers several agencies to help protect consumers from unscrupulous lenders and collection practices. The Federal Trade Commission (www.ftc.gov) is a good source for information about national consumer protection laws. Your state attorney general (www.naag.org/attorneys_general.php) and local Better Business Bureau (www.bbb.org) can offer help closer to home.

If you haven't been able to work out acceptable terms with your creditors and the overdue notices and collection agency calls are mounting, your next best option is to contact a credit counseling agency. But read the next paragraph *very carefully* before you make that call.

First, as consumer debt problems have mushroomed, credit counseling has grown into a huge for-profit industry. Legitimate credit counselors attempt to negotiate lower interest rates and workable payment plans with your creditors, for a fee typically paid *by* the creditors. Many unscrupulous firms, however, charge consumers ridiculously large fees or percentages of total debt, and some simply collect a high sign-up fee then skip town. Check with your local Better Business Bureau before signing an agreement or handing over any money to a credit counseling firm.

Debt Consolidation

	Current Balance	Interest Rate	Annual Charges and Fees	Monthly Payment	Length of Loan (Months)
Debt Account 1	$ 1,000	15.00%	$ 25.00	$184.48	12
Debt Account 2	$ 500	21.00%	$ 50.00	$116.86	12
Debt Account 3	$ 1,250	18.00%	$ -	$260.78	12
Debt Account 4	$ 900	12.00%	$ -	$145.29	12
Debt Account 5	$ 200	12.00%	$ 15.00	$37.54	9
Debt Account 6	$ 125	15.00%	$ -	$23.06	12
Totals				$768.02	
Debt Consolidation Loan	$3,975	14.00%	50	$702.26	12
Difference between Old Debt and Consolidated Loan				$65.76	

Most (legitimate) agencies will devise some sort of debt consolidation plan, which folds all of your outstanding debts into a single payment, typically at a lower interest rate than you're currently paying. But wait! You might be able to do this same consolidation maneuver on your own, if you have a loan source that will lend you money for a lower interest rate than you're paying to your creditors. Maybe you can ask a friend or family member for an interest-paying loan, or perhaps you can borrow against your retirement account at work (check with your Human Resources representative). To see how a debt consolidation loan might work, use the Debt Consolidation worksheet to compare your current payments and interest rates to a single payment at a lower rate.

The Least You Need to Know

◆ Managing debt requires that you manage your use of credit cards. Cut most of them up and leave the others at home when you go out. You can't get out of debt if you keep adding to it!

◆ Failing to pay secured debts can result in the loss of your collateral—and that collateral could be your home or car.

◆ Refinancing a major loan to achieve lower monthly payments can pay off, but only if the new interest rate is lower and the loan fees are reasonable.

◆ Lenders use your credit report and score to determine whether to lend you money and how much interest to charge you for the loan. Excessive debt and late payments are fast ways to harm your credit history.

◆ If you haven't been able to reduce your debt effectively, consolidating all of your debts into one payment at a lower interest rate might be a solution.

◆ Carefully research any credit counseling service before putting your financial recovery plan in their hands.

Chapter **7**

Managing Your Insurance— and Your Risks

In This Chapter

◆ Is your health insurance healthy?

◆ Betting on the right life insurance coverage

◆ Insuring your worldly goods

◆ Do you need disability insurance?

◆ Maintaining a less-than-risky existence

Buying insurance of any kind is the equivalent of making a bet that something bad is going to happen to you. These wagers add up, too (there's a reason they call insurance payments "premiums"). Unlike feeding the nickel slots, however, insuring your health, life, and property is just good common sense. Bad things *do* happen, and they can change your life in sudden and unpredictable ways. Insurance is your best bet for dealing with the financial costs of adversity.

Insurance is expensive and choosing the right type of coverage is a tricky business. I've designed the worksheets in this chapter to make the job easier and more cost-efficient. From comparing health insurance policy benefits, to choosing the right type and amount of life insurance coverage, to controlling costs for home, auto, and personal property coverage, this chapter can help you make the right insurance choices. And here's my promise: no agent will call, write, or e-mail.

As your lifestyle and income change, so do your insurance needs. Be sure to regularly revisit the worksheets in this chapter to determine that your insurance coverage keeps up with your life!

Relief from the Headache of Health Insurance Choices

When you're young and unemployed, health insurance is an easy thing to shrug off. As you move on into your thirties, though, and you have a job, a spouse, maybe a child or two, the thought of "what might happen" makes you look more closely at the options offered by your employer's health insurance program. That is, *if* you're lucky enough to have those options. If you're footing the bill solely on your own, you'll have even tougher choices to make, as you try to find the health insurance coverage you need at a price you can afford.

Making the Right Choice

All insurance plans have limitations: You agree to pay a *deductible* before the insurance kicks in. You have a *co-pay*, and the insurance picks up the rest. You see the doctor you want, or you see a doctor the insurance company tells you to see. In spite of their massive variability, however, most insurance plans fall within a few basic forms. Here are the two most common:

def•i•ni•tion

A **deductible** is the amount of money you have to pay for specified insured events or services before the insurance company benefits come into effect. A **co-pay** is the set amount you pay, as defined by your insurance, for every doctor's visit or medical event.

- **Fee-for-service** plans pay you a percentage of your medical service fees, after you meet your deductible. See who you want, go to the hospital of your choice. These plans are expensive—and increasingly rare in employer-offered plans.

- **Managed care** plans, to varying degrees, limit your medical providers to those on the insurer's approved provider list. You pay a co-pay for every approved visit, the plan picks up the rest. One doctor typically manages your care, by referring you to other specialists within the organization, as appropriate. Health Maintenance Organizations (HMOs), Point-of Service, and Preferred Provider plans fall within this category. The latter two enable members to receive some level of reimbursement for seeing doctors outside the plan.

Costs and limitations vary dramatically between providers and among types of policies. Think carefully about your family history, current health, and lifestyle when determining which options are critical, and which you can pass by. A few general guidelines apply to most of us:

♦ If you're young and single, opt for the highest deductible you can afford. You're minimizing your guaranteed costs, for a slightly elevated risk. At minimum, you need coverage for major medical incidents.

♦ If you have a chronic health condition, go for a lower deductible and a large lifetime limit on costs. Be sure, however, to find out how long the plan excludes coverage for *preexisting conditions*. Go to www.healthinsuranceinfo.net to find your state's health insurance rules and guidelines.

♦ Don't shell out big bucks for dental coverage. If it's automatically included in your employer's plan, great. Otherwise, it's cheaper to pay for your own cleanings and checkups. Again, however, you must keep your own dental condition and family situation in mind when making this decision.

♦ Do your research. Health insurance is too costly and important for snap decisions. Ask questions of your Human Resources department, talk to friends about their coverage and experiences, and read *carefully* the details of any policy you're considering.

def•i•ni•tion

A **preexisting condition** is any medical condition you've been treated for during a set period of time prior to enrolling in an insurance program. That period could be six months or longer, depending on the provider and the state in which you live.

Comparing Health Insurance Plans

A thoughtful comparison of policy offerings and restrictions is the only way you can determine which type of policy is right for you. When you've narrowed the field to a few options, gather up the policy descriptions, and then use the Health Insurance Benefits Comparison worksheet to see how the policies you're considering stack up against each other.

Health Insurance Benefits Comparison

Health Insurance Plan	Policy A	Policy B	Policy C
Monthly premium (fill in amount)			
Deductible or co-pay (fill in amount)			
Maximum benefit limits (fill in amount)			
Coverage for pre-existing conditions (check if yes)			

Medical Service (check all that apply)	Policy A	Policy B	Policy C
Hospital care			
Surgery (inpatient and outpatient)			
Office visits to your doctor			
Emergency room visits			
Exclusions			
Well-baby care			
Immunizations			
Screenings such as mammograms and pap smears			
Medical tests and x-rays			
Mental health care			
Dental care, braces, and cleaning			
Vision care, eyeglasses, and exams			
Prescription drugs			
Home health care			
Nursing home care			
Maternity care			
Choice of doctors			
Location of doctors and hospitals			
Consumer ratings			
Drug and alcohol abuse			
Chiropractic and alternative healing services			

Smoking Cessation/Health Club Benefits	Policy A	Policy B	Policy C
Annual limits for days or services covered and the amount spent on you			
What is the maximum you will have to pay out-of-pocket each year			
What is the lifetime limit, if any, that you will be reimbursed			

Smoking Cessation/Health Club Benefits	Policy A	Policy B	Policy C
Annual limits for days or services covered and the amount spent on you			
What is the maximum you will have to pay out-of-pocket each year			
What is the lifetime limit, if any, that you will be reimbursed			

You need expert guidance when choosing a health-care plan. Many states and consumer organizations offer ratings for health insurance plans. Visit www. consumerhealthratings.com to learn more. Or visit www.kiplinger.com, click The Basics tab at the top of the home page, then choose Insurance to access well-written and unbiased articles on health insurance options and issues. Finally, the Joint Commission on Accreditation of Healthcare Organizations (www.jointcommission. org) and the National Committee for Quality Assurance (www.ncqa.org) offer great guides to choosing and assessing health-care plans.

The Facts of Life Insurance

None of us likes to think about the world going on without us, but it will. That's why we buy life insurance—to protect our assets and provide for those we leave behind. Use the worksheets in the following sections to help determine whether you need life insurance, and (if so) what type and amount of coverage you should look for.

Is It Really Necessary?

Now, not all of us need to worry about life insurance. Not because we won't die—sorry, no exemptions there—but because we simply won't leave anyone in a financial lurch if we ... you know ... "check out" sometime soon. Okay, rather than stare into the great void of eternity, let's do something more useful. Ask yourself the following questions to determine whether you need to worry about life insurance now.

- ◆ Are you young and single, with no dependents?

    If you answered Yes, you don't need life insurance, and can move to the next topic in this chapter. If you answered No, read on.

- ◆ Do you live with a spouse or partner who depends on your income to meet expenses?

    If you answered Yes, you need at least enough life insurance coverage to pay for your funeral expenses and to provide for your missing income for six to nine months. (By the way, your spouse or partner needs life insurance to protect *you*, too.)

- ◆ Do you have children or other dependents?

    If you answered Yes, in addition to the insurance needs listed above, you need enough life insurance to help with tuition, home care, and other expenses.

◆ Do you own a business that a partner or family member may want to carry on?

If you answered Yes, in addition to any other demands on your life insurance, you need to be sure you have enough to cover cash flow, estate taxes, debt, and other expenses.

? In the Know

If you have elderly parents with limited financial means, you might want to consider carrying a life insurance policy that lists them as the beneficiaries. Money won't lessen their grief after you're gone, but it will help make their lives a bit easier by providing them with some financial security in your absence.

What Type? How Much? Choosing Life Insurance Coverage

Like any financial instrument, there are more varieties and flavors of life insurance than any one person could ever need. But all life insurance falls within two broad categories: term life insurance and permanent life insurance.

Term life insurance provides a simple death benefit for as long as you pay the policy premium. Term insurance has the lowest cost of entry, and is a good temporary or short-term choice of coverage. With annual renewable term, the premium rises each year. Extended term policies come with a guaranteed steady premium and death benefit for a specific period of time, after which the premium rises. (Avoid extended term insurance that requires evidence of insurability to renew beyond the original extended term.)

Permanent life insurance accumulates funds as you pay premiums. As the amount grows, you can cash it in or borrow against it. Permanent life insurance is a sensible purchase if you intend to hold on to the policy throughout your life. Permanent policies come in three varieties:

def•i•ni•tion

Term life insurance pays a benefit when you die, and that's it. You can't cash it in or borrow against it. **Permanent** life insurance, on the other hand, makes a portion of your premium payments available to you down the road, should you want to forget about your dependents, cash in your policy, and live it up (while you still can).

◆ *Universal* life insurance involves a range of premium payments. These policies offer a cash accumulation feature, for those who pay more than the required minimum premiums. While agents often sell these policies as a great way to force savings, they aren't great savings vehicles.

◆ *Variable universal* life insurance places your cash value accumulation in a series of separate accounts of your choosing. Separate accounts in a life insurance or annuity contract function similarly to mutual funds and may contain stocks, bonds, or any other investment classes, as defined by their prospectus. The owner of the policy can decide which of the many choices to use. Again, however, poor implementation and oversight often makes these accounts lackluster investment vehicles.

◆ *Whole-life* insurance is for those who intend to hang on to the policy throughout their lifetime. The annual premium for whole-life is high in the beginning and relatively lower in later years. Cash accumulations earn a low rate, similar to a savings account or CD. Many whole-life policies have a cash-surrender value (CSV), which is the amount of money you will receive if you cancel the policy.

The life insurance salesperson will sometimes tug at your emotions, and ask you to consider how much you love someone when determining the amount of coverage to have. Don't fall for that line. No matter how much your emotions might play a role in choosing a coverage amount, you can determine how much life insurance you truly *need* by using basic math.

How much Social Security death benefits will your heirs be eligible for? How much debt will you leave behind? Will your family need a lump sum of money, just to deal with immediate expenses after your death? Do you have children who will need childcare and college tuition? How many years will your heirs need financial support? Use the Life Insurance Needs Calculator to enter projections based on these and other important financial questions, and to calculate the amount of life insurance you should carry.

> **? In the Know**
>
> If your stay-at-home partner who currently cares for your children would return to work after your death, your life insurance coverage should include the cost of childcare. These costs vary, of course, but the National Association of Child Care Resource and Referral Agency offers a state-by-state table of average costs at its website (www.naccrra.org).

Life Insurance Needs Calculator

Annual Survivor Living Expenses		$250,000
Subtract:	Survivor Earnings	$47,000
	Other Annual Death Benefits	$15,000
Annual Income Replacement Need		**$188,000**
Number of Years to Fund Income Shortfall		12
Total Survivor Living Expenses Need		$188,000
		$2,256,000
Add:	Lump Sum Needs	$50,000
	Costs at Death	$9,000
	College Funding	$75,000
	Debt Payoff	$25,000
	Child Care	$22,000
	Retirement Fund Supplement	$40,000
	Estate Taxes	$251,000
		$472,000
Total Capital Needed		**$2,728,000**
Subtract:	Existing Life Insurance	$150,000
	Current Savings and Investments	$250,000
		$400,000
Net New Life Insurance Need		**$2,328,000**

Insuring Your Stuff: Homeowner's, Renter's, and Automobile Insurance

As you begin to accumulate possessions, you are wise to begin protecting them, as well. Many people, especially when just establishing a career and financial stability, could suffer a dramatic economic setback if they lost all of their possessions in a fire or totaled their car. And, even the bravest squirms at the idea of being the subject of a personal injury lawsuit. No, it's much easier to pay insurance premiums than to try to bail out in the aftermath of a disaster.

That doesn't mean, however, that you should drain your bank account in the process of insuring your home and possessions. Let's take a look at what types of policy options you do (and don't) need when insuring your most important assets.

Homeowner's and Renter's Insurance

Don't worry about having to make the decision to insure your home. Most mortgage lenders insist that you do. No bank wants to hold the mortgage on an uninsured house that was carried away in a tornado.
Homeowner's insurance covers the costs of damage to the dwelling itself as well as its contents—your sofa, your refrigerator, your shoes, your eight-season DVD collection of *The Sopranos*. Homeowner's policies also provide liability coverage. If your dog bites the mailman or if someone trips over your doorsill upon arriving at your housewarming party, your homeowner's policy should cover the cost of their injuries.

In the Know

If you run a business from your home, you may need a special rider to cover accidents and losses related to that business. Ask your insurer for full details.

Don't own a home? Well, then, you need protection for everything that's in your rented space. Renter's insurance covers your possessions and provides that ever-important liability coverage as well. As with all insurance, homeowner's and renter's policy offerings vary among companies and coverage levels. Here are the most important details to look for:

- **Replacement cost:** The policy should reimburse you for the price you would pay to replace your damaged assets. You'll be paying full cost for the replacement goods you buy, so that's what your insurance should provide.

- **Liability coverage:** Your homeowner's or renter's policy should cover the costs of your legal liability for personal or property damage involving your property. Many policies top out at $300–$500K, which may not be enough if someone wins a hefty liability lawsuit against you. If your policy doesn't include it, consider adding on ....

- **Umbrella Liability Coverage:** This add-on takes care of expenses above the limit of regular liability coverage. It typically runs about $200–$300 a year for up to $1 million or $2 million of liability coverage. Umbrella coverage provides valuable protection against lawsuits leveled against you in the wake of an accident on or involving your property. You will be thrilled to have this coverage if one of your trees falls on a neighbor's restaurant quality Viking outdoor grill (while he's using it).

◆ **Medical coverage:** The policy should provide for the medical costs of a guest who is injured on your property. If your dog bites someone while you're away from home, ditto—your homeowner's/renter's medical coverage should provide adequate payment for their treatment.

◆ **Loss of use:** The policy should cover many living costs incurred when you have to move out of your home during covered repairs—hotels, meals, laundry, and so on. Check to make sure you know the details of this coverage in any policy you're considering.

Comparison shopping is essential when tracking down the homeowner's or renter's policy that's right for you. Many policies exclude certain types of coverage, such as damage caused by earth movement, flood or sewer backup, or acts of war. Use the Property Insurance Policy Checklist to determine if any policy you're considering meets your needs.

Property Insurance Policy Checklist

☐　Does the policy provide replacement costs for personal property?

☐　Does the policy provide earthquake coverage?

☐　Does the policy provide flood coverage?

☐　Do you conduct business from the home?

☐　Does the policy include necessary coverage for jewelry, art, or other valuables you own?

☐　Does the policy cover contents of your refrigerator and/or freezer?

☐　Does the policy cover personal property not stored at home?

☐　Does the policy cover all computer equipment at the insured home?

☐　Does the policy cover any boat, trailer, or other RV you have stored at your home?

☐　Does the policy provide adequate coverage for garages, sheds, or other structures on your property?

☐　Does the policy provide personal umbrella liability coverage?

☐　Does the policy cover the property of your children who are away at school?

Pitfall Alert! _____

> After buying a policy, check it carefully for accuracy. Be sure that you've insured your property for the proper amount. Check that the policy's named insured matches the name on your deed or rental agreement and that the property and mailing addresses are accurate. If you have a mortgage, be sure the mortgage holder's name and account number are accurately listed.

After you have asked yourself all of the checklist questions regarding the policies that you're considering, use the Homeowners/Renters Insurance Policy Cost and Exclusions Comparison worksheet to compare the premiums, deductibles, and limits of the final contenders.

Homeowners/Renters Insurance Policy Cost and Exclusions Comparison			
	Company A	Company B	Company C
Premium			
Deductible			
Exclusions			

Insuring Your Ride

Most states require that you carry automobile insurance, so you really can't afford to shrug off this essential coverage. It's expensive, so your best bet is to find the most affordable policy that meets your needs, and to carry the highest deductibles you can handle. In most cases, the higher your deductible, the lower your premium. Also, be aware that many companies offer policy discounts based on the features of your car, such as anti-lock brakes, theft protection, airbags, and so on. Your age or driving habits may qualify you for a discount, as well. When you're comparing policies, be sure to ask about any and all available discounts, so you're comparing the best rates you can get.

Here are the essential elements of an automobile insurance policy:

◆ **Property Damage Liability** covers damage you (or someone driving your car with your permission) cause to someone else's property, whatever that property might be (a car, a fence, a garage, and so on).

◆ **Collision** pays for damage to your car resulting from an accident. It also covers damage caused by potholes. Collision coverage is generally sold with a deductible of $250 to $1,000.

◆ **Comprehensive** reimburses you for loss due to theft or noncollision damage—fire, falling objects, earthquake, windstorm, hail, flood, vandalism—and from contact with animals such as birds or deer. It also provides coverage for cracked or shattered windshields. This coverage typically carries a $100 to $300 deductible.

◆ **Uninsured and Underinsured Motorist Coverage** reimburses you for repairs if your vehicle is hit by an uninsured motorist, or if an at-fault driver has insufficient insurance to pay for your total loss. This coverage also applies if you are hit as a pedestrian.

◆ **Bodily Injury Liability** coverage applies to injuries to someone else. Drivers listed on the policy are also covered when driving someone else's car with their permission.

In the Know

States do not require that you purchase collision or comprehensive coverage, but if you have a car loan, your lender may insist you carry it until your loan is paid off.

◆ **Medical Payments or Personal Injury Protection (PIP)** pays for the treatment of injuries to the driver and passengers of the policyholder's car. At its broadest, PIP can cover medical payments, lost wages, and the cost of replacing services normally performed by the injured person—it might even cover funeral costs (but let's hope that's not necessary).

Just as you did when comparing health insurance benefits, use the Automobile Insurance Comparison worksheet to determine what discounts each auto policy offers, and what limits they place on benefit amounts.

Buying Disability Insurance

Unless you have a magic cape of invincibility hanging in your closet, you really need to think about how you would manage financially if you were unable to work. Many employers offer disability insurance policies for little or no additional cost to employees. If you have access to one, grab it. Otherwise, consider buying one on your own. Every insurance company has its own definition of disability. And, of course, you need to review the guidelines and stipulation governing when, how, and for how long any policy pays benefits. Some will pay when you are unable to do your current work, while others will pay only if you are unable to do *any* work.

Automobile Insurance Comparison			
Basic Policy Costs/Reimbursements (fill in amounts)	**Policy A**	**Policy B**	**Policy C**
Premium			
Deductible			
Replacement Rental Car Reimbursement			
Available discounts for which you're eligible (check all that apply)	**Policy A**	**Policy B**	**Policy C**
Accident Prevention Course			
Passive Restraint Devices			
Anti-Lock Brakes			
Anti-Theft Devices			
Driver Training			
Multi-Car Discount			
Retiree/Senior Citizen			
Reduced Driving Discount			
Daytime Running Lights			
Other			
Limits (fill in amounts):	**Policy A**	**Policy B**	**Policy C**
Liability			
Bodily Injury			
Medical Payments			
Property Damage			
Collision			
Comprehensive			
Underinsured or Uninsured Motorist Coverage			

Many insurance companies offer individual and business policies. If you're self-employed or a part-time worker, you might be eligible for disability insurance at group rates through a professional organization you belong to, such as the Author's Guild or the National Teacher's Association.

So how much disability insurance do you need? A broad rule of thumb says that you need a monthly amount equal to your after-tax take-home pay (plus any contributions you make to a 401K or other pension plan). You might be able to shrink that amount, however, if you take into consideration any other sources of income you might be

Pitfall Alert! _____

Choosing insurance coverage is an important step, and that's doubly true when you're talking about health, life, and disability coverage. Before you make these important decisions, get the facts from a more complete reference. See Appendix B for some book suggestions.

Pitfall Alert! _____

Social Security Disability Insurance and Supplemental Security Income will provide some baseline coverage if you become disabled, but need to be considered supplements to your own disability insurance coverage.

eligible for during the period of your disability. Your employer's health plan may include some disability insurance, and you may be eligible for Social Security benefits as well (the Social Security Statement you receive annually outlines your eligibility and payment amounts).

Gather this information, along with your basic monthly living expenses. You calculated these in Chapter 3, but you may need to revise the amounts, if your expenses could be expected to change if you became disabled. When calculating the full amount of disability benefits, remember to take into consideration any waiting period required by your policy, along with the policy's maximum length of coverage. Finally, remember that Social Security benefits may change, and will only apply should you become unable to perform *any* job for which you're qualified.

With this information in mind, use the Disability Insurance Calculator to help determine how much financial help you might need in the event of a long-term mental or physical disability.

Analyzing (and Managing) Risks

As you've probably gathered, life is all about managing the risks you can't avoid. Insurance is an important step in that direction—it's your safest haven in the wake of personal or financial disaster. Managing your exposure to risks also involves understanding exactly how exposed you really are.

Think about the unthinkable. If you use a wireless phone or Internet connection, you might be more vulnerable to eavesdroppers or hackers who can gain access to your electronic information. If you travel frequently, you may need to think about how well your property is protected during your absence, or how you would handle a devastating illness or accident while you're on the road. If you have hired workers at your home or conduct business from a home office, you may need to discuss your added liability with an insurance agent. Do you really understand the insurance coverage you have for your residence, vacation home, or your most valuable possessions?

Disability Insurance Calculator

Total Basic Monthly Living Expense*	$ _____
Less:	
Estimated Income from Disability Income Policies** in place	
Personal coverage	$ _____
Coverage from work	$ _____
Social Security Disability Income	$ _____
Other	$ _____
Net Income Shortfall	$ _____
Less:	
Income from savings and investments	$ _____
Net Income Shortfall during Disability	$ _____

* Consider the effect of a disability on expenses. Certain expenses may decrease as a result of disability and other expenses may increase or be created.

** Consider the waiting period and duration of all benefits received.

By contemplating your lifestyle and the risk factors it involves, you can better prepare to sidestep the risks you can avoid and to deal with those you can't. The Risk Analyzer worksheet, used with the permission of the Chubb Group of Insurance Companies, provides a helpful tool for profiling your risk factors. Answer the simple Yes and No questions, then consider the implications of your answers. You might determine that you need to change some of your current practices, adopt new ones, or have a nice long talk with your insurance agent.

Risk Analyzer

Identity Theft:	Y	N
Do you or your family use the Internet for personal business?		
Does any third party have access to your personal information (accountant, attorney, banker, domestic employees, etc.)?		
Do you utilize up-to-date anti-virus and anti-spyware programs on all computers in your home?		
Do you utilize wireless technology (laptop, phone, camera, etc.)?		
Does your personal liability policy include coverage for identity theft?		
Do you know the appropriate steps to take if you are a victim of identity theft?		

Travel:	Y	N
Do you or any family member travel outside of the United States?		
Do you travel domestically or internationally more than three times per year?		
Do you have medical evacuation coverage if you become injured or ill overseas?		
Does someone reside at or check daily on your residence while you are traveling?		
Is your home protected by a central station burglar alarm?		

Personal Liability:	Y	N
Do you employ domestic staff such as a housekeeper or nanny?		
Do you serve as a director, officer, or member of the board for a public, private, and/or non-profit organization?		
Do you conduct business from your home?		
Do you make statements to the press?		
Do you know how much liability coverage you have?		
Have you updated your liability limits regularly to reflect your personal net worth?		

Personal Security:	Y	N
Do you have children?		
If yes, are they at home or away at school? Y=Home N=School		
Do you worry about personal security risks such as home invasion, child abduction, or carjacking?		
Do you have insurance coverage for personal security threats to you or your family?		

Personal Residence:	Y	N
Has your residence been appraised for its insurance replacement value?		
Do you know the amount your insurer will pay for a total loss to your home?		
Do you have flood insurance for your residence?		
Do you own a secondary residence?		
Has your agent presented you with various deductible options and the estimated savings for these options?		

Valuable Possessions:	Y	N
Do you know how your insurance would respond if your personal property were damaged or destroyed?		
Do you collect jewelry, fine art, silver, or other fine possessions?		
Do you have dedicated insurance coverage (a valuable articles policy) for the items you collect?		
Do you maintain a thorough inventory of your valuable possessions?		

Personal Risk Management:	Y	N
Do you review your insurance coverage with your agent on an annual basis?		
Do you currently work with a captive agent or broker such as State Farm or Allstate (vs. an independent agent or broker)?		

The Least You Need to Know

- Even if you don't feel that you need (or want) to carry health insurance to pay for every sniffle and scrape, you need to carry enough health insurance to cover major medical problems.

- Life insurance is designed to cover the necessary expenses and income needs of your partner, dependents, or other ongoing responsibilities after your death.

- Most mortgage holders require you to carry homeowner's insurance, and most states require you to carry automobile insurance.

- Most homeowner's, renter's, and automobile insurance policies include liability coverage. If that coverage has low limits, consider adding on umbrella liability coverage.

- Disability insurance has you covered if you become incapable of working, due to either a mental or physical impairment. Disability insurance is relatively affordable, and a good idea.

Chapter 8

Giving the Tax Man His Due (and Not a Penny More)

In This Chapter

◆ Making a tax-saving plan

◆ Keeping good records

◆ Weighing the differences between "tax-free" and "tax-deferred"

◆ A taxpayer's guide to Roth and traditional 401K plans

Before you slam this workbook shut and run screaming from the room, let me assure you of one important fact: this chapter is *not* about how to fill out and file your tax forms, nor is it a guide to the history of taxation in the United States. A full-blown explanation of our tax system and its much-reviled paperwork would occupy an entire book, all on its own. And there are many of those books out there (for a lean and saving-of-the-green guide to taxes, might I suggest *The Complete Idiot's Guide to Personal Finance in Your 20s & 30s, Fourth Edition*, or see Appendix B for more print and online resources for taxpayers). The focus of *this* chapter of *this* book, however, is trained squarely on minimizing the amount of income tax you pay, by maximizing the deductions and other tax breaks that are rightfully yours.

The tools in this chapter help you in that effort in a number of ways, from reducing your taxable income and testing multiple tax-planning strategies, to comparing the benefits of taxable and tax-free bonds and choosing a 401K plan that will maximize your actual benefits. The worksheets and planning tools in this chapter will help you do your part as a loyal American taxpayer, while protecting the home front right where it counts the most—in your wallet.

Minimizing Your Taxes

When we talk about minimizing your taxes, what we're really talking about is reducing your taxable income by maximizing your deductions, tax credits, and tax-free or tax-deferred savings. You might think that the percentage of your income that goes to taxes is determined by your *tax bracket*, but that's not necessarily so. If you've ever paid taxes in the past, you might remember that this is how the process shakes out:

1. Add up your total gross income.

2. Subtract all adjustments, such as retirement plan contributions, some IRA contributions, student loan interest payments, and so on, to determine your *adjusted gross income*, or AGI.

3. From your AGI, subtract your exemptions (one for you, one for each dependent, at a current rate of $3,500 each).

4. From the remainder, subtract your deductions, either standard or itemized, to determine your *taxable income*.

5. Look at the current tax table to determine the amount of taxes due for the tax bracket your income places you in.

6. From the taxes due amount, subtract any credits you have coming, such as child credits, energy efficiency credits, and so on.

7. To the remainder, add any other taxes you might owe, such as taxes on premature IRA distributions, to determine your total tax debt for the current year.

8. Subtract from your total tax debt the taxes your employer withheld from your wages, or any estimated tax payments you made, to determine how much tax you still owe, or how much of a refund you have coming back.

Now, you might have noticed that there's a lot more subtracting than adding going on in that process, and that's good news. But you don't want to be one of the tens of thousands of American taxpayers who fail to make the most of those subtractable moments in the tax calculation process.

def•i•ni•tion

Your **adjusted gross income** (AGI) is the amount of all the money you earned in a given year, minus allowable adjustments. Your **taxable income** is your AGI, minus personal exemptions and standard or itemized deductions. Your taxable income puts you into a **tax bracket**, which determines what percentage of your income you must pay in income tax. Rates currently run between 10 and 35 percent.

The Income Tax Reduction worksheet guides you through a variety of options for reducing your income taxes by deferring income or by increasing deductions and their benefit on your tax return. Don't think we're talking small potatoes, either. If you're in a 15 percent tax bracket (which currently means you're single and have taxable income somewhere between $7,825 and $31,850 a year according to the 2007 tax tables), increasing a 401K or IRA contribution by $2,000 a year will save you approximately $350 in taxes. If you donate $5 a week to your church, write a check instead and save $40 per year in taxes. Or let's say that you give your favorite charity $1,000 every year. Instead of writing a check for $1,000, consider donating shares in a mutual fund that you've owned for a while. If you pay $700 for the shares, and by the date of the contribution, the value of those funds has risen to $1,000, you get to claim that full appreciated value as your deduction. That means your charitable gift gave a little something back to you!

The variable that determines just *how much* these items can save you is your tax bracket (you can find the current tax bracket tables in any IRS income tax form, or online at www.irs.gov). With your individual income and tax bracket information in place, you can use the Income Tax Reduction worksheet to enter a wide variety of tax-reducing variables and calculate the potential tax savings. You can then funnel your tax reductions right into your cash flow forecast.

In the Know

It pays to know your tax credits—sums you can subtract directly from the amount of taxes you owe in repayment for any number of actions the state or federal government wants to encourage. There are credits available for everything from donating a kidney to having a baby or buying an energy efficient dishwasher. Learn more about tax credits at www.irs.gov.

Income Tax Reduction

Deductions:

Retirement plan contribution	$2,500
Re-finance points	$2,500
State tax payments otherwise due when filing	$0
Military Reserve travel expenses	$2,500
Out of pocket for charity	$0
Total Deductible	**$7,500**

Credits:

Child care	$50
Hybrid auto	$4,000
Foreign tax credit	$0
Credit for the elderly or disabled	$550
Total Credit	**$4,600**

Opportunities:

Gifting to charities	$400
Gifting appreciated properties	$1,500
Establishing an IRA	$2,000
Establishing a self-employed retirement plan	$3,000
Home office deduction	$2,500
Medical savings account	$4,500
Educator expenses	$12,000
Mileage for charities	$1,500
Donations of property or clothing	$750
Job expenses	$1,200
Misc. tax deductions that exceed 2% of AGI	$1,450
Energy savings home improvements	$450
Total	**$31,250**

Keeping Track

One of your best bets for coming out ahead at tax time is to keep accurate records and receipts for deductible expenses. Those expenses include some medical and educational expenses, mortgage and other loan interest, property taxes, charitable contributions, and unreimbursed job costs—and that's a partial list.

Keeping accurate records and receipts is doubly important if you are self-employed and/or run a home-based business. When your financial life is relatively simple, you'll probably take the standard deduction (currently $5,450 for a single individual, $10,500 for married couples filing jointly). But as your income—and deductible expenses—go up, so does the likelihood that you'll want to itemize deductions. Then, you'll be glad you developed the habit of tracking your deductible expenses throughout the year.

Tax-Free or Tax-Deferred?

Many decisions related to minimizing your taxes (and maximizing your income) will involve choosing opportunities to invest part of your income in tax-free or tax-deferred holdings. If you put some of your money in tax-deferred holdings, such as a 401K or other retirement plan, U.S. Treasury bills, or bonds, for example, you won't have to pay taxes on that investment until you begin to draw it out (at retirement or when you cash in the bills or bonds). Tax-free income, however, isn't subject to Federal tax at all, and may be exempt from state and local taxes, as well.

Municipal bonds are one example of a tax-free investment. You can buy these bonds, issued by a number of cities around the United States, and they will pay interest—typically a modest amount, mind you. But, that interest is tax-free, so you don't have to pay federal, state, and in some cases, local taxes on it (you learn more about bonds and the tools for working with them in Chapter 10).

It can be tough to determine just which of these tax-sheltered options pays the biggest benefit, however. Is it more lucrative, for example, to earn 4 percent interest on a tax-free bond, or to earn 5 percent interest on a tax-deferred investment, and pay the taxes when you cash in the investment? Or should you buy taxable bonds now, pay the tax, and gain a bigger yield down the road? Making these decisions can be tough, and that's why you'll be glad to have the Taxable versus Tax-Free Bond Analysis worksheet. This table calculates the outcomes of buying tax-free or taxable bonds, based on your tax bracket, the bonds' interest rates, and withdrawal restrictions. Plug in the variables for investments you're considering, then let the worksheet calculations determine which bonds will give you the greatest *after-tax yield* or income.

def•i•ni•tion

After-tax yield refers to the rate of interest you receive on an investment after taxes have been calculated and subtracted.

Taxable versus Tax-Free Bond Analysis

	Taxable	Tax-Free
Amount invested	$10,000	$10,000
Interest Rate	4.00%	3.00%
Tax Rate on Interest	25%	0%
After-Tax Yield	3.00%	3.00%

> ### ? In the Know _____
>
> Before you read further, go grab your tax return from last year and force yourself to look it over. Now, imagine that there's a new column to the right of all of those line items, and it's titled "What If?" As in: "What will it do to my taxes if I get a $5,000 raise?" or "What if I itemized my deductions?" That "What if" line could help you determine the potential future tax implications of any number of actions. You can play the "What If?" game using tax preparation software such as TurboTax. All of the electronic tax preparation software packages have modules that are relatively easy to use for this purpose.

Socking Money into a Roth or Traditional Retirement Plan

One of the most common ways that Americans minimize taxable income is through 401K retirement plans. You might be contributing to one even as we speak (see Chapter 14 for more information and worksheets to help you with setting up retirement accounts and distributions). In a 401K plan, you make regular contributions, based on an amount that you determine. Your employer may or may not add their own contribution to your account, depending upon how the plan is structured. Like most investments, the money you sock into your 401K should grow as your investments appreciate, and all of that lovely money is there waiting for you when you retire. The market's imperfections are vast, of course, but with the demise of most company-sponsored pension plans, 401K plans have become the best option for many Americans.

> ### ? In the Know _____
>
> You've probably heard about traditional and Roth Individual Retirement Account (IRA) plans. These plans share most of the same benefits and restrictions as the traditional and Roth 401K plans discussed in this chapter. You learn more about IRAs in Chapter 14.

401K plans come in two varieties, traditional and Roth. In a traditional 401K, your contributions are tax-deferred. You get to deduct the full amount of your contribution from your income today, thereby reducing your taxable income and income tax bill. You pay taxes on the money later, when you withdraw it at retirement.

Roth 401K plans are *not* tax-deferred. You pay income tax on your contributions at your regular income tax rate. The beauty of these plans blooms later. You can withdraw from them at any time at retirement age, *and* you never owe taxes on the money you withdraw—not even on the appreciation or interest from your investment! So, if you invest $10,000 this year in a Roth 401K, and that investment is worth $40,000 when you withdraw it, you pay no taxes on the extra $30,000 in your account.

Although, in general, Roth 401Ks are better choices for young savers who anticipate that they'll have worked their way into a higher income tax bracket by the time they retire, this isn't necessarily so. If you contribute $5,000 into a traditional 401K plan this year, for example, your income is reduced before taxes by $5,000. If you are in a 20 percent tax bracket, you save $1,000 in taxes, right off the bat. If you want to invest $5,000 in your Roth 401K plan this year, however, you will use $6,250 of your taxable income to end up with that $5,000 in the plan (again, if you are in a 20 percent tax bracket). If you can spare that tax money today, however, you're very likely to make it back (and then some) down the road when you withdraw from the Roth. Your withdrawal will then be totally tax-free money—including all of the appreciation on your original investment.

If you're fighting off a finance-induced trance right now, take a deep breath and look at the Traditional versus Roth 401K Calculator. You can use it to calculate the immediate financial consequences of choosing either type of 401K plan. Simply enter the amount of money you want to put into your 401K this year, then enter your tax bracket information. The worksheet will calculate the immediate tax consequences of investing your chosen amount in a traditional or a Roth 401K.

In the Know

For a complete rundown on Roth 401K plans, visit www. roth401kinfo.com. This site has great information and killer tools for your retirement calculations.

Traditional versus Roth 401K Calculator

	Roth	Traditional
Amount withheld from paycheck per year	$ 5,000	$ 5,000
Income tax bracket	25%	25%
Tax savings with Traditional	▮▮▮▮	$ 1,250
Tax cost of Roth	$ 1,250	▮▮▮▮
After-tax total cost of contribution	$ 6,250	$ 3,750

The Least You Need to Know

- You can trim your taxes (sometimes substantially) by taking all of the deductions, adjustments, and other tax breaks you have coming to you.

- Planning ahead is the best way to get the most tax savings. Test scenarios for contributions, delayed income, and other options, when choosing the most financially beneficial approach.

- Keep accurate records and receipts for all tax-deductible expenses.

- Tax-deferred income is money you earn today but pay taxes on later, when you withdraw it from your tax-deferred investment. Tax-free investments save you money in taxes, but typically pay a lower interest rate.

- A traditional 401K retirement plan lets you avoid paying taxes on your contributions until you actually begin withdrawing from the plan. Roth 401K plans hold after-tax investments, but benefit you later, by paying out tax-free earnings.

Part 3

Accumulating Wealth: Savings and Investment

Okay, you know how to protect your stash, but now it's time to learn how to make it grow. In this part of the book, we dive into the timely topic of savings and investment.

After a quick run through the basics (and some killer tools for mastering them), you'll be ready to tackle the meatier issues of asset appreciation—where to invest your money, how to evaluate your current investments, and how to make sure they continue to give you the best returns.

Do you have a 401K? Are you contributing to an IRA? Do you have a savings account or a CD? No matter how new you are to the world of investing, or how basic your current savings plan might be, the tools and strategies in Chapters 9 through 12 will help you get the highest return for every dollar that you save. (And that's how you get to the 'happily ever after' part of your life story.)

9

Savings and Investment Basics

In This Chapter

- ◆ Determining your risk tolerance
- ◆ Estimating the size of your nest egg
- ◆ Savings plan starters
- ◆ A first look at investment basics

Over the past few years, the path toward a safe financial future has seemed a bit, shall we say, rocky. Even the most savvy investment analysts have found themselves stumbling over their attempts to balance the fundamental need to protect their investments with their burning desire to score double-digit earnings growth. The sorry lesson we all learned in the global economic turmoil of 2008 was an old one: what goes up must come down, and the higher up that teetering earnings ladder you climb, the harder and more devastating your fall can be.

What the wisest among us also learned, however, was that a savings plan coupled with a smart approach to investment are essential for building a sound financial future. In this chapter, you learn how to use some important tools for managing the first part of that equation. From gauging your tolerance for risk to evaluating savings accounts and understanding the most basic types of investments, the questionnaires, charts, and spreadsheets in this chapter will give you a solid start on the economic journey ahead.

Gauging Your Tolerance for Risk

As a kid, I was something of a daredevil—first to hop on the roller coaster, first to try the rope swing, first to try to befriend every stray dog that wandered into the neighborhood. Some of these risks were stupid, but all of them taught me important lessons about consequences. And those are some of the most important lessons any of us can learn.

Today, my work is all about sizing up financial risks and weighing the potential rewards and punishments that might result from them. I can advise my clients on those potential outcomes, but I can't tell them how they will react to them. Each of us has to determine just what consequences we're willing to suffer in order to achieve our own unique financial goals. You don't have to depend on guesswork to size up your risk tolerance, either. The following Risk Tolerance Questionnaire will help you determine your own risk threshold, and it will even give you a head-start toward determining what kind of savings and investment portfolio fits your risk tolerance profile.

In the Know

Conservative investors prefer to hold a lot of their money in cash, rather than in stocks or bonds. The older you are, the more conservative your investment plan might be. Younger people have a longer time to hold and adjust their investments, and can follow a more aggressive plan by investing heavily in stocks.

It's easy to use. For each question, circle the answer that seems best to you. Then, use the table that follows the questionnaire to assign a value to each answer and arrive at a total score for the questionnaire. For example, if you choose answer D for question 3, you'll add 4 points to your total score. After you've calculated your total score, refer to the Answer Key to see where your score places you on the "conservative to aggressive" investment plan continuum. The Answer Key even outlines a possible portfolio mix of stocks, bonds, and cash for each of five score ranges.

Risk Tolerance Questionnaire (RTQ)

PLEASE READ FIRST: The Risk Tolerance Questionnaire is an evaluation tool only. Please **CIRCLE** the letter that best corresponds with your answer to each question.

1. **As an investor, where would you place yourself on the following risk scale?**
    A. I want to minimize risk and avoid investment value fluctuation.
    B. I am willing to tolerate some risk and investment value fluctuation.
    C. I am willing to tolerate more risk and investment value fluctuation for a greater return.

2. **What is your age?**
    A. Under 25
    B. 25 to 34
    C. 35 to 44
    D. 45 to 54
    E. 55 to 65
    F. Over 65

3. **How many years remain until you retire?**
    A. More than 30 years
    B. 20 to 30 years
    C. 11 to 19 years
    D. 6 to 10 years
    E. 0 to 5 years

4. **Is your spouse currently enrolled in a Retirement Plan [e.g., 401(k) or 403(b) Plan]?**
    A. Yes
    B. No
    C. Presently not married

5. **Do you expect to have additional cash needs for your future security other than retirement? (Such as buying a home, paying for college education, having a health-related expense.)**
    (Early withdrawal may be subject to a 10% penalty if you are less than 59½ years old.)
    A. No
    B. Yes, in 16 to 20 years
    C. Yes, in 10 to 15 years
    D. Yes, in 5 to 9 years
    E. Yes, in less than 5 years

6. **Does this statement reflect you: "I am willing to tolerate short-term fluctuations in the value of my investments in order to gain a potentially higher return over a long period of time"?**
    A. Strongly agree
    B. Agree
    C. Neutral
    D. Disagree
    E. Strongly disagree

7. **Which statement best reflects your investment objective and time-frame for achieving it?**
    A. Investing for long-term security for 20 years or longer
    B. Investing for a time frame of 10 to 19 years
    C. Investing for a time frame of 5 to 10 years
    D. Investing for a time frame of 2 to 5 years
    E. To preserve the capital and provide income in the immediate future

Setting Your Financial Expectations

I'll talk about retirement planning in detail in Chapter 14, but in reality, planning for retirement is nothing more than planning for the future. And that's what saving and investing are all about. And, as you've undoubtedly heard before, you can never start planning too soon.

Your goal should be to have a healthy nest egg set aside in some kind of investment that earns enough interest to keep you going (your nest egg should supply you with approximately 70 percent of your current income after retirement). If you have a $500,000 nest egg, for example, and it earns a fixed rate of 5 percent interest, then it will provide you with $25,000 per year of interest income.

The longer you have to save and invest, the more your nest egg can grow. Your contributions aren't the only fertilizer for that growth, either. Compounding plays an important role in building your financial stash. When your savings and investment vehicles offer *compounded interest*, the dollar you invest today earns a return, and at specific periods (daily, weekly, monthly, quarterly, or annually) that interest also earns interest. Over the years, all of those compounded returns add up to more money for you.

def•i•ni•tion

When your savings or investment vehicle returns **compounded interest,** you earn interest not only on your original deposit, but also on the accumulated interest that deposit earns over time. Periodically, the balance is calculated to add accumulated interest. At each recalculation period, the total balance (original deposit plus all previously earned interest) earns interest. That's how your money grows!

So how much money will you need when you retire? Although that amount varies dramatically with your circumstances, tastes, interests, and abilities, most experts recommend that you estimate your needs based on a hypothetical expense plan that reflects the lifestyle you want to lead during your retirement. Even with Social Security and a pension plan, you may need a good investment return to match a lifestyle that's currently fueled by a six-figure income.

You can see how important it is that you save and invest wisely today. Where you save and invest your money determines what kind of earnings you can achieve. Historically (at least over the past 100 years), cash saved in money markets, Treasury bills, and other cash reserves has earned just under 4 percent a year. Over the same period, government bonds have pulled in approximately 5 percent a year, and stocks have returned an average of 10 percent per year according to most sources. Those are just averages, of course, but they give you some idea of the kind of returns that historically have resulted from these common types of investments. By all means, however, please remember that past performance is not indicative of future results.

All of this matters a lot when you're deciding just how much money you need to save for the "happily ever after" part of your life. To get some sense of how these rates of return can affect your financial outcome, take a look at the next two worksheets. The Fixed Rate of Return Nest Egg Estimator shows you a hypothetical retirement scenario for somebody who starts with a relatively cushy setup. This person, who we'll call Bill Ginner, expects to have access to some healthy assets when he retires. His parents own a commercial building that he plans to sell after he inherits it. His pension plan is in place and on track to supply about $18K a year after he retires. He also plans to continue with some consulting work for at least the first few years of his retirement, and he'll have some Social Security income, as well.

He's taken all of that information and plugged it into the Fixed Rate of Return Nest Egg Estimator, along with his best estimate of what annual income he'll need in retirement. He (like you) can estimate that inflation will grow by about 4 percent every year during his retirement (that should be a bit high, but it's a safe planning number). Bill also estimates that his income will grow at a slightly higher rate of 5 percent every year. The Estimator uses all of this data to show how Bill's nest egg will hold out if it returns a fixed rate of 4, 6, 8, or 12 percent interest. Plug in your own expectations and estimates to see how your financial future might unfold, based on these fixed rates of returns on your investments.

In our example, look what happens to Bill's nest egg as the years go by. At age 81, he could start sinking into a financial hole if his investments are returning a fixed rate of 4 percent. At 6 percent returns, he can keep operating in the red until he hits age 88, and if he's lucky enough to get 12 percent on his investments, he's good until the (exceptionally) ripe old age of 125!

That future scenario will hold if Bill is invested in CDs or money-market funds that pay a fixed rate of return. But if Bill's investments are heavily loaded into stocks or variable annuities (see Chapter 10) that vary in the rate of return they offer, his future becomes much more, well, variable. Look at the Variable Rate of Return Nest Egg Estimator, to see how his Nest Egg balance might fluctuate, based on those variable returns.

Now, you can't predict how variable returns will fluctuate over the years, but this estimator gives you some sense of how dramatically variable rates of return can shape your financial future. And both of these estimators do a good job of helping you set realistic expectations for how much money you'll need down the road, so you can craft a savings and investment plan that will fit those needs.

Fixed Rate of Return Nest Egg Estimator

My Name	**B. Ginner**
Date	06/23/09
Assets Available for Nest Egg *	**$3,000,000**
Retirement Age	60
Required Retirement Income	**$250,000**

Income Sources

Part-time Income	Please input in the table below
Social Security Retirement Income	24,000
Pension	18,000
Other Income	6,000
Total Income	**$48,000**
Estimated Income Growth Rate	**5.0%**
Expected Annual Expense Inflation	**4.00%**

Note: * This total should only include assets you will apply toward retirement. Do not include assets such as real estate or personal property unless you intend to sell the asset and use the proceeds for retirement

					Nest Egg Balance with Rate of Return @			
Year	Age	Required Income	Part-Time Income	Fixed Annual Income	4.00%	6.00%	8.00%	12.00%
1	61	-$250,000	**$50,000**	$48,000	$2,909,920	$2,965,880	$3,021,840	$3,133,760
2	62	-260,000	**50,000**	50,400	2,808,333	2,921,657	3,037,219	3,275,059
3	63	-270,400	**25,000**	52,920	2,694,487	2,866,427	3,045,318	3,424,489
4	64	-281,216	**25,000**	55,566	2,567,590	2,799,224	3,045,242	3,582,699
5	65	-292,465	0	58,344	2,426,809	2,719,010	3,036,011	3,750,408
6	66	-304,163	0	61,262	2,271,263	2,624,675	3,016,558	3,928,408
7	67	-316,330	0	64,325	2,100,029	2,515,030	2,985,717	4,117,571
8	68	-328,983	0	67,541	1,912,130	2,388,803	2,942,217	4,318,864
9	69	-342,142	0	70,918	1,706,542	2,244,633	2,884,672	4,533,356
10	70	-355,828	0	74,464	1,482,185	2,081,065	2,811,573	4,762,231
11	71	-370,061	0	78,187	1,237,923	1,896,542	2,721,274	5,006,800
12	72	-384,864	0	82,096	972,562	1,689,402	2,611,988	5,268,517
13	73	-400,258	0	86,201	684,845	1,457,865	2,481,765	5,548,995
14	74	-416,268	0	90,511	373,451	1,200,035	2,328,489	5,850,026
15	75	-432,919	0	95,037	36,992	913,881	2,149,855	6,173,601
16	76	-450,236	0	99,789	-325,994	597,240	1,943,360	6,521,932
17	77	-468,245	0	104,778	-717,039	247,799	1,706,284	6,897,481
18	78	-486,975	0	110,017	-1,137,758	-136,909	1,435,672	7,302,985
19	79	-506,454	0	115,518	-1,589,842	-559,516	1,128,314	7,741,494
20	80	-526,712	0	121,294	-2,075,071	-1,022,830	780,727	8,216,405
21	81	-547,781	0	127,358	-2,595,313	-1,529,848	389,129	8,731,500
22	82	-569,692	0	133,726	-3,152,530	-2,083,763	-50,583	9,290,999
23	83	-592,480	0	140,413	-3,748,781	-2,687,980	-542,863	9,899,603
24	84	-616,179	0	147,433	-4,386,228	-3,346,129	-1,092,537	10,562,560
25	85	-640,826	0	154,805	-5,067,139	-4,062,079	-1,704,843	11,285,724

26	86	-666,459	0	162,545	-5,793,895	-4,839,953	-2,385,458	12,075,627
27	87	-693,117	0	170,672	-6,568,994	-5,684,142	-3,140,535	12,939,564
28	88	-720,842	0	179,206	-7,395,056	-6,599,325	-3,976,745	13,885,679
29	89	-749,676	0	188,166	-8,274,828	-7,590,485	-4,901,315	14,923,069
30	90	-779,663	0	197,575	-9,211,193	-8,662,927	-5,922,075	16,061,899
31	91	-810,849	0	207,453	-10,207,173	-9,822,303	-7,047,509	17,313,523
32	92	-843,283	0	217,826	-11,265,935	-11,074,626	-8,286,804	18,690,633
33	93	-877,015	0	228,717	-12,390,802	-12,426,299	-9,649,910	20,207,416
34	94	-912,095	0	240,153	-13,585,254	-13,884,135	-11,147,600	21,879,731
35	95	-948,579	0	252,161	-14,852,939	-15,455,387	-12,791,540	23,725,310
36	96	-986,522	0	264,769	-16,197,680	-17,147,769	-14,594,357	25,763,983
37	97	-1,025,983	0	278,007	-17,623,483	-18,969,490	-16,569,720	28,017,928
38	98	-1,067,022	0	291,908	-19,134,542	-20,929,281	-18,732,421	30,511,950
39	99	-1,109,703	0	306,503	-20,735,252	-23,036,430	-21,098,471	33,273,800
40	100	-1,154,091	0	321,828	-22,430,216	-25,300,815	-23,685,194	36,334,521
41	101	-1,200,255	0	337,919	-24,224,253	-27,732,940	-26,511,332	39,728,847
42	102	-1,248,265	0	354,815	-26,122,412	-30,343,973	-29,597,164	43,495,645
43	103	-1,298,196	0	372,556	-28,129,973	-33,145,790	-32,964,628	47,678,406
44	104	-1,350,124	0	391,184	-30,252,470	-36,151,013	-36,637,454	52,325,802
45	105	-1,404,129	0	410,743	-32,495,689	-39,373,063	-40,641,306	57,492,307
46	106	-1,460,294	0	431,280	-34,865,691	-42,826,201	-45,003,945	63,238,888
47	107	-1,518,706	0	452,844	-37,368,815	-46,525,586	-49,755,391	69,633,790
48	108	-1,579,454	0	475,487	-40,011,693	-50,487,327	-54,928,107	76,753,402
49	109	-1,642,632	0	499,261	-42,801,267	-54,728,540	-60,557,197	84,683,234
50	110	-1,708,337	0	524,224	-45,744,795	-59,267,412	-66,680,615	93,519,016
51	111	-1,776,671	0	550,435	-48,849,872	-64,123,267	-73,339,398	103,367,913
52	112	-1,847,738	0	577,957	-52,124,439	-69,316,630	-80,577,913	114,349,909
53	113	-1,921,647	0	606,855	-55,576,801	-74,869,308	-88,444,122	126,599,330
54	114	-1,998,513	0	637,198	-59,215,641	-80,804,461	-96,989,873	140,266,577
55	115	-2,078,454	0	669,057	-63,050,039	-87,146,688	-106,271,211	155,520,042
56	116	-2,161,592	0	702,510	-67,089,485	-93,922,116	-116,348,715	172,548,276
57	117	-2,248,055	0	737,636	-71,343,901	-101,158,488	-127,287,866	191,562,399
58	118	-2,337,978	0	774,518	-75,823,655	-108,885,265	-139,159,432	212,798,812
59	119	-2,431,497	0	813,243	-80,539,585	-117,133,729	-152,039,900	236,522,225
60	120	-2,528,757	0	853,906	-85,503,013	-125,937,095	-166,011,931	263,029,059
61	121	-2,629,907	0	896,601	-90,725,772	-135,330,625	-181,164,856	292,651,244
62	122	-2,735,103	0	941,431	-96,220,222	-145,351,755	-197,595,210	325,760,480
63	123	-2,844,507	0	988,503	-101,999,275	-156,040,225	-215,407,312	362,773,013
64	124	-2,958,288	0	1,037,928	-108,076,421	-167,438,220	-234,713,886	404,154,971
65	125	-3,076,619	0	1,089,824	-114,465,744	-179,590,516	-255,636,735	450,428,357

Pitfall Alert!

The potentially devastating results of downturns in variable rates of returns are the primary reason that most experts advise that you take the most risks when you're young, and have plenty of time to recover from losses. As you age, most advisors recommend that you choose investments that are safer and less vulnerable to the ups and downs of the marketplace.

Variable Rate of Return Nest Egg Estimator

My Name	B. Ginner
Date	06/23/09
Assets Available for Nest Egg *	$3,000,000
Retirement Age	60
Required Retirement Income	$250,000

Income Sources	Age 60 -65	Age 66 -70	Age 71 +
Consulting Fees	$50,000	$20,000	$0
Social Security Retirement Income	24,000	24,000	24,000
Pension	18,000	18,000	18,000
Other Income	6,000	0	0
Total Income	**$98,000**	**$62,000**	**$42,000**

Estimated Income Growth Rate	5.0%
Expected Annual Expense Inflation	4.00%

Note: * This total should only include assets you will apply toward retirement. Do not include assets such as real estate or personal property unless you intend to sell the asset and use the proceeds for retirement

Year	Age	Required Income	Annual Income	Annual Rate of Return	Nest Egg Balance
1	61	-$250,000	$98,000	7%	$3,047,360
2	62	-260,000	102,900	-2%	2,832,455
3	63	-270,400	108,045	9%	2,910,409
4	64	-281,216	113,447	14%	3,126,610
5	65	-292,465	119,120	-7%	2,746,536
6	66	-304,163	79,129	11%	2,798,868
7	67	-316,330	83,086	6%	2,719,561
8	68	-328,983	87,240	12%	2,775,157
9	69	-342,142	91,602	5%	2,650,847
10	70	-355,828	96,182	22%	2,917,266
11	71	-370,061	68,414	-3%	2,537,150
12	72	-384,864	71,834	-7%	2,068,432
13	73	-400,258	75,426	12%	1,952,832
14	74	-416,268	79,197	4%	1,680,392
15	75	-432,919	83,157	10%	1,463,693
16	76	-450,236	87,315	-4%	1,056,741
17	77	-468,245	91,681	4%	707,384
18	78	-486,975	96,265	25%	395,841
19	79	-506,454	101,078	-7%	-8,867
20	80	-526,712	106,132	-2%	-420,859
21	81	-547,781	111,439	17%	-1,002,925
22	82	-569,692	117,010	15%	-1,673,948

23	83	-592,480	122,861	**6%**	-2,272,180
24	84	-616,179	129,004	**8%**	-2,980,104
25	85	-640,826	135,454	-6%	-3,276,347
26	86	-666,459	142,227	15%	-4,370,666
27	87	-693,117	149,338	11%	-5,455,034
28	88	-720,842	156,805	7%	-6,440,406
29	89	-749,676	164,645	-1%	-6,955,182
30	90	-779,663	172,878	12%	-8,469,404
31	91	-810,849	181,522	14%	-10,372,554
32	92	-843,283	190,598	-5%	-10,473,978
33	93	-877,015	200,128	9%	-12,154,443
34	94	-912,095	210,134	14%	-14,656,300
35	95	-948,579	220,641	6%	-16,307,293
36	96	-986,522	231,673	-1%	-16,891,521
37	97	-1,025,983	243,256	7%	-18,911,446
38	98	-1,067,022	255,419	-4%	-18,934,127
39	99	-1,109,703	268,190	18%	-23,335,256
40	100	-1,154,091	281,600	4%	-25,176,057
41	101	-1,200,255	295,680	8%	-28,167,084
42	102	-1,248,265	310,464	12%	-32,597,472
43	103	-1,298,196	325,987	5%	-35,248,165
44	104	-1,350,124	342,286	7%	-38,793,923
45	105	-1,404,129	359,400	-4%	-38,245,106
46	106	-1,460,294	377,370	11%	-43,654,112
47	107	-1,518,706	396,239	-5%	-42,537,750
48	108	-1,579,454	416,051	18%	-51,567,361
49	109	-1,642,632	436,853	-9%	-48,023,557
50	110	-1,708,337	458,696	-5%	-46,809,539
51	111	-1,776,671	481,631	14%	-54,839,220
52	112	-1,847,738	505,712	7%	-60,113,932
53	113	-1,921,647	530,998	-2%	-60,274,490
54	114	-1,998,513	557,548	14%	-70,355,619
55	115	-2,078,454	585,425	1%	-72,567,134
56	116	-2,161,592	614,696	9%	-80,784,291
57	117	-2,248,055	645,431	-4%	-79,091,439
58	118	-2,337,978	677,703	15%	-92,864,471
59	119	-2,431,497	711,588	17%	-110,663,724
60	120	-2,528,757	747,167	8%	-121,440,938
61	121	-2,629,907	784,526	-2%	-120,820,593
62	122	-2,735,103	823,752	9%	-133,777,819
63	123	-2,844,507	864,940	16%	-157,478,568
64	124	-2,958,288	908,187	7%	-170,695,676
65	125	-3,076,619	953,596	8%	-186,644,194

Sound Ideas for Savings

When you're young, you may not have a lot of money, but you have lots of time to accumulate more. Sure, you might make a killer investment that lands you a big wad of dough, but the most reliable tool you have for building a big stash of cash is a regular and systematic savings plan. I know that saving money isn't the sexiest idea you've toyed with lately, but it might be the most useful thing you can do with your youth.

Throughout Parts 1 and 2 of this book, I talked about a number of ideas for saving money, from cutting back on everyday expenses to eliminating credit card debt. But not spending the money is only step one in saving. The second step is actually putting that saved money somewhere safe. At least part of those savings should be socked away in a savings account that gives you ready access, when necessary, to your cash.

Where and how you save makes a difference. Every bank offers various levels of savings accounts, which typically fluctuate in the amount of interest they pay, the minimum amount of deposit they require, and the fees charged for ATM, live teller access, and other services. When you're shopping around for a good savings account for your cash, you need to compare all of these factors so you make the choice that's right for you. Use the Savings Account Evaluator to list and compare your savings options.

Savings Account Evaluator

Bank	Interest Rate	Minimum Term Required	Minimum Account Size	Monthly Fees		Other Features and Benefits
NoRisk Farmers Bank Money Saver	3.60%	None	None	$	5.00	Unlimited free withdrawals; no fees
Mutual Fidelity S&L Silver Level Savings	5.60%	None	$2,000	$	-	Unlimited free withdrawals; online access to account
Safe Harbor Money Market Fund	8.10%	16 months	$5,000	$	7.50	Three free withdrawals a month

? In the Know _____

Don't forget that in savings accounts, as in life, every benefit has a cost. Higher interest rates typically demand higher minimum deposits and—in some cases— limited free services. If you think you're going to be dipping into your account frequently, you might be better off taking a lower interest rate, if it means you can avoid extra usage costs or minimum balance penalties.

First Steps in Savings and Investing

No matter how wildly the investment picture may change on occasion, as I mentioned earlier, the younger you are, the more heavily you should depend on systematic savings for building your nest egg. I'll talk in detail about planning and managing your investments in the chapters ahead, but for now, let's just take a look at some common beginner's investment choices—some of which you may already be holding.

Length of Investments

Investments typically come in three forms. Long-term investments are those that you expect to last for 10 years or longer. Stocks fall into this category, as do some mutual funds. The idea behind these investments is that their value may rise and fall dramatically with the market but, in the end, investors hope for growth and higher returns. Mid-term investments are those you expect to hold for 3 to 10 years. These investments might include stocks combined with more conservative mutual funds and bonds. Short-term investments (fewer than three years) offer the lowest risk, and include interest-bearing savings accounts, certificates of deposit, and FDIC guaranteed money-market accounts. These investments give you quick access to your funds with a small return in interest. Before you embark on any investment plan, however, you should build an emergency fund with enough money to carry your basic expenses for three to six months. That fund should be with you throughout your adult life—and that's a really long haul!

The Most Common Investments

Almost everyone who is working has some basic forms of investment. Here are some of the most common:

- ◆ **Mutual funds** are the pooled contributions of a number of investors. The funds are invested in stocks, bonds, and other holdings, and managed by a team of financial experts who are responsible for making wise investment decisions. Because you're teaming up with a number of other investors, you share the risks—and costs—of investing. Mutual funds enable you to diversify your investment holdings and benefit from professional management, which is good. They also enable you to set up a monthly investment plan, which will sock your money away before you have a chance to spend it on something less "future-worthy."

- **Money-market funds** are similar to money-market accounts offered by banks, but these funds are managed by mutual fund companies, and they aren't insured by the FDIC. Yes, you can lose money on them, but most mutual funds work hard to make sure that doesn't happen. These accounts are relatively safe, depending upon the safety of the investments within the funds. Money-market mutual funds strive to have a dollar-for-dollar investment value, meaning that if you put in $1, you expect to get $1 back, along with the interest paid by the mutual fund company for that particular fund.

- **Certificates of deposit, or CDs,** are offered by financial institutions as secure investment vehicles. These institutions typically require that you deposit a minimum amount of money for a minimum amount of time—six months, a year, five years, and so on—with longer times offering higher interest rates. At the end of the specified time, the bank pays you your original deposit along with the interest rate it's earned. If you take money out before the specified time, you have to pay a penalty.

> **? In the Know**
>
> You aren't taxed on the money you contribute to a traditional 401K plan until you withdraw it. That means that even though your income is reduced by the amount of your contribution, your tax burden also goes down. Your postretirement tax bracket may be lower, too, which means you'll pay less tax overall than you would have had you not invested in the plan.

- **401Ks** have replaced the traditional employer-sponsored retirement plan. In these plans, the company offers a wide range of investment choices that you, the participant, get to choose from. Employees can contribute part of every paycheck to the plan, and in some cases, the employer also contributes to each employee's account. If you leave the company before retiring, you can roll your investments into another 401K or roll them over into an IRA. When you retire, you can withdraw the money without penalty (as long as you are older than 59½). You get to choose from among a number of investment options within your 401K plan, and you can change your portfolio "mix" at set periods throughout the year.

Take a moment right now to determine just how much of your income you're currently saving and investing. In the Savings and Investment Estimator, list your current monthly or annual contributions to savings and investment accounts. Type in your monthly or annual pretax gross income, and the estimator will calculate the percentage of your income that you're currently saving. Most experts recommend that you try to save at least 10 percent of your income each year. How close are you to that goal?

Savings and Investment Estimator

Your Annual Savings Source	Annual Savings Amount
401K	$10,000.00
IRA	$5,000.00
Funds deposited to a savings account	$2,000.00
Direct deposits into investment accounts	$1,500.00
Other	$500.00
Other	$1,000.00
Other	$750.00
Total Annual Savings Amount	$20,750.00
Total Pre Tax Gross Income	$75,000.00
Savings as a Percentage of Gross income	28%

All of the investment vehicles you've just read about are relatively low-risk. That means that, if you're young, you also may want to consider taking on some riskier (and potentially more rewarding) investments. You learn about doing just that in Chapter 10.

The Least You Need to Know

- Everyone has a unique tolerance for risk. You need to understand your own risk tolerance and create a savings and investment plan that fits it.

- You should try to build a nest egg that will provide you with approximately 70 percent of your current income after retirement, but remember that Social Security, pension plans, and part-time work can contribute to your postretirement income.

- By drawing compounded interest, your savings can grow dramatically over a 10, 20, or even 30 year period.

- When you invest in CDs, mutual funds, money-market accounts, or a 401K, you've made the first steps on the road toward a financially sound future.

10

Where Should You Invest?

In This Chapter

- ◆ A blueprint for the do-it-yourself stock portfolio
- ◆ How to be a smart bond buyer
- ◆ Investing in mutual funds
- ◆ Annuities demystified

There once was a time when state and local governments debated whether to allow ordinary citizens to pump their own gas—too great a risk of fuel spills, explosive fires caused by careless smoking, and other cataclysms, many warned. Today, we live in a self-service world. On any given day, somebody is selling their own home, buying airline tickets online, monitoring their own blood-sugar levels, and managing numerous other tasks that they used to leave up to the "pros." It's only natural, therefore, that we've also had to step up to the financial planning plate and take at least some responsibility for choosing our own investments.

I'll be honest with you: this chapter involves some heavy lifting. If you aren't interested in buying individual stocks, bonds, and annuities, you might want to go directly to the section on investing in mutual funds, and then move on to the next chapter. If you're considering individual investments, read the other sections and consider—very carefully—the questions and comparisons they offer. In any event, the tools and charts in this chapter won't prepare you to become the chief financial advisor to the Getty Charitable Trust, but they will help you lose any lingering fear and intimidation you may have about diversifying your 401K or choosing a well-managed mutual fund. Being in charge of your investment choices is much, much better than living in fear of them. And I promise—no explosive fires will result!

Building a Stock Portfolio

This workbook isn't the place to give you grounding in the intricate workings of the stock market. In fact, I assume that you already have formed a basic understanding of the stock market before you begin considering buying individual stocks within it. I offer a fast and lean rundown of the market here, but it's only going to provide a couple of base points for what is a very involved playing field.

When you buy stock, you're actually buying ownership shares in the company that issued the stocks. As the value of the company rises, so does the value of its stock. You make money on stocks by selling them after they have increased in value, and/or through annual *dividends*, which are payments the company makes to its stockholders, based on the company's profits for that year.

def•i•ni•tion

A **dividend** is a payment to stockholders, issued by a company, based on the company's profits for that year. Most dividends are paid on a quarterly or annual basis.

The Dow Jones Industrial Average (DJIA) tracks the performance of stocks in a key group of 30 companies that are considered (by *The Wall Street Journal* and stock investors everywhere) to be a representative index of the United States' overall economy. The Standard and Poor's (S&P) 500 is an index of 500 stocks that investors also consider to be representative of the U.S. economy. These indexes are published regularly, and give you a good profile of the overall health of the market.

Okay, so what about investing in this market? Well, as I've said in earlier chapters of this book, individual stocks are among the riskiest investments you can make. And yet, many investors consider stocks to be essential elements in any young person's long-term investment plan. Why?

In spite of its up and down gyrations, historically, the stock market has given investors a greater return on their investment dollars than have less volatile choices such as bank accounts or money-market funds. As you learned in the last chapter, over the past century, stocks have returned an average of almost 11 percent growth annually.

But remember those gyrations. In 2002, the market dropped by nearly 24 percent. By 2007, it had risen again to hit an historic high. And then it plummeted in September of 2008, losing nearly $6 billion of investor wealth in a single day, before beginning a slow crawl upward again. The lesson here is that most stock investments should be considered in terms of the long haul time horizon. I'll define long haul at 5 to 10 years or longer. You don't want to have to sell your stocks to raise cash if the timing for that sale isn't right. You want your investment to have time to ride out the market's highs and lows as it builds in value.

Most beginning investors choose to use a broker or to buy into a mutual fund that chooses and buys stocks for a large pool of investors (you learn more about mutual funds later in this chapter). Alternatively, you can buy individual stocks online, using any one of the many online sellers of securities. But be aware of the risks involved, and remember that stocks are best viewed as long-term investments, not as a source of short-term rewards.

Pitfall Alert!

Even the savviest stock traders fail to get in and out of the market at the right time, every time. If you decide to dabble in individual stock trading, prepare to spend a lot of time educating yourself on your picks. And set a limit for the amount of money you'll sock into it. That way, even when you lose, you won't lose everything.

If you do want to invest directly in stocks, I recommend that you buy what you know. In other words, if you're a medical technician, you might be interested in investing in a pharmaceutical firm or in a medical supply company whose products you know and trust. If you work in a restaurant, you might know quite a bit about up-and-coming wineries or restaurant equipment manufacturing companies that would offer good investment potential. Even your own shopping habits or knowledge of emerging consumer trends might shape your investment choices. This isn't to say that your personal preferences will influence the stock market. And, it's important that you maintain a diversified stock portfolio, with stocks from a range of industries and market sectors, so that a downturn in any one area (such as the tech bubble that burst in the late 1990s) won't take your whole stock portfolio down in flames. But if you know or work with companies that are respected in your field or industry, those companies may make good first moves for you as you begin investing in the stock market.

If you're going to invest directly in stocks, here are my six tips for doing it wisely:

1. **Set goals for your portfolio and let them guide your choices.** This is a long-term investment, and you can't let day-to-day fluctuations send you into a panic.

2. **Do your homework.** First, consider investing in businesses or industries that you know something about. Then, before you invest in a company's stock, read the company's business plan and the annual report it must file every year with the Securities and Exchange Commission (this information should be available on the company's website). The annual report to stockholders will show you the low and high prices for the company's stock over the past year, its dividend history, and major initiatives that might impact its stock value. Also, consider how competitive this company is within its field and marketplace.

3. **Diversify your portfolio.** Nothing stays "hot" forever, so don't limit your investments to any single industry or market sector (finance, technology, real estate, pharmaceuticals, energy, and so on). The more you diversify, the better your chances of surviving market downturns and benefiting from overall market growth.

4. **Create an investment plan and stick with it.** Determine what percentage of your stock holdings you want to invest in any stock you're considering. Set a sell price at both ends of the pricing spectrum. One at the lowest price at which you're willing to still own a stock and one where you think that your profit objectives have been met. Determine ahead of time, for example, whether you're willing to hold the stock if it drops by 20 percent in value.

5. **Don't get carried away.** If you sell all of your stock holdings during a downturn, you'll be selling low and may lose money. Buying stocks when the market is low actually gives you a good shot at scoring returns when the market eases back up. At the same time, you don't want to bulk up on high-return (and high-risk) stocks during the market's good times. If you do, you may be buying high and could pay big-time when the market's exuberance cools. Again, remember ups and downs are part of the market, so a steady, systematic investment plan is best.

6. **Find a good advisor and check in with him or her often.** Getting good advice from a financial pro is the way to go if you're interested in investing in the stock market. But even then, you need to meet regularly with that person to make sure your investment plan still matches your goals.

Now, if you're considering making any stock investment, use the Stock Buyer's Guide to help vet your choices before you buy. Consider and answer each question, then evaluate how well your answers stack up. Make sure you have positive—and sound— answers for each question before you take the plunge.

Stock Buyer's Guide

Stocks	Question	Answer
	How long am I willing to own this stock?	
	What criteria am I using to select this stock?	
	What sector does this stock represent?	
	What percentage of my portfolio is represented by similar holdings?	
	Do I have a target price to lead my decision to sell this stock?	
	Do I understand what this company does?	
	Does the business plan for this company sound plausible?	
	Have I read the annual report and the SEC filings 10K and 10Q?	
	Is there broad institutional ownership for this stock?	
	Will this stock pay dividends?	
	What is the 12-month low and high price for this stock?	
	Would I keep this stock if the price dropped by 20% next month?	
	Does this stock add to the desired balance and allocation in my overall portfolio?	
	Is this company a market leader with their products or services?	
	In what ways is this company materially different from its competitors?	

Owning Individual Bonds

When you buy stocks, you're buying (small) pieces of ownership in a company. When you buy bonds, however, you're actually loaning your money to the entity that issued the bond. Companies issue corporate bonds, the federal government issues Treasury bonds, banks can issue their own bonds, and state and city governments can issue municipal bonds. The bond issuer, in turn, agrees to pay you interest semi-annually and repay you the principal on a specific date when the bond matures.

Bonds come with an advertised interest rate—what is called the bond's *yield* or *coupon*. The bond's *yield to maturity* is the amount of all of the returns it yields. Most bonds pay yields twice a year. Interest rates can change, of course, which can have an impact on the value of your bond (if new bond interest rates go up, your bond becomes less valuable). You pay taxes on those earnings, of course, unless they come from tax-free bonds (you learned about tax-free municipal bonds back in Chapter 8). U.S. Treasury bonds, for example, are typically considered to be quite safe, although they don't pay sky-high yields.

Bonds arc rated (for the issuer's ability to pay the interest and repay the principal in a timely manner) by organizations such as S&P and Moody's. These ratings range from AAA, which is the highest rating, to D, which represents a bond that few beginning investors should even consider. Bond ratings, yields, and *maturity* periods are posted along with stock market information, or you can check them online using a tool such as Yahoo!'s Bond Screener (http://bonds.yahoo.com/safety.html).

As with stocks, individual bond investment isn't for the faint of heart. If you're intent on making this kind of investment, you might want to think about starting with what many folks consider to be your safest bet—U.S. Treasury bonds. You can buy them from a bank or through a broker, or you can buy them directly from the Treasury by visiting their website (www.savingsbonds.gov/). If you decide to go ahead with other types of individual bond investments, however, you'll need to purchase the bonds from a broker—and that includes all of the online brokerage firms who spend millions on advertising trying to get your money. But before you do that, use the Bond Buyer's Guide to make sure you understand what you're investing in—and why. Like the Stock Buyer's Guide you used earlier in the chapter, ask yourself some questions and make sure your answers add up to a compelling case for making the investment.

def•i•ni•tion

A bond's **yield** or **coupon** is the interest it pays on the original investment. The **maturity** date is the date when your loan will be repaid by the bond issuer, and it can be anywhere from 3 to 30 years. The **yield to maturity** represents all of the returns you realize from the bond.

Buying Mutual Funds

You can save yourself a lot of time on the investment learning curve by buying into mutual funds, which you first learned about in Chapter 9. Mutual funds gather up the investment dollars of a large pool of investors, and then invest those dollars in a selection of stocks, bonds, and other securities. That's one of the great advantages of investing in a mutual fund—you get the distinct advantage of having a professional advisor manage your investment choices. Mutual funds also spread the costs and risks of investment among a large pool of investors. This allows for low costs and a diversified portfolio chosen by professionals who make it their full-time job to find the most lucrative investments. What more could you want?

Bond Buyer's Guide

Bonds	Question	Answer
	What is the safety rating of the bond issuer?	
	What is the current yield to maturity for this bond?	
	When does this bond mature? Am I planning to hold this bond to maturity? Is this bond taxable or tax free?	
	How does the income from this bond compare to a very low-risk bond such as a U.S. Treasury bond or a money market fund?	

There are three common types of mutual funds you might invest in:

◆ **Stock funds:** Managers of these funds pull together a collection of stocks that represent a specific profile for investors—*Blue chip* stocks, *value* stocks, *growth* stocks, small companies, international companies, and so on. Some funds focus strictly on specific industries, specific sizes of companies, or specific geographic regions. All offer a full description of their focus and historic returns, so you can study up on the fund before buying in. Buying stock funds gives you the benefit of that all-important professional fund management, and it's considered a less risky way to invest in the stock market because of the broad diversification and many holdings inside most funds, as opposed to the limited portfolio that can result from making a few individual stock purchases on your own.

def•i•ni•tion

Blue chip stocks are those of well-established companies such as General Electric, Exxon Mobil, and so on. **Growth** stocks are those of companies whose mission is to grow by exploring new markets, products, or other opportunities. **Value** stocks are stocks deemed inexpensive relative to other similar stocks or the company's operating profits or asset base.

- **Bond funds:** These collections of bond investments are considered less volatile than stock funds. Bond fund managers tinker with their bond holdings, however, so you don't just get and hold a specific set of bonds until their maturity date. These funds are good choices when you don't need to pull out all of your principal investment on a specific date, and prefer instead to just collect the dividend payments earned by the funds' collective bonds.

- **Money-market funds:** These funds are similar to a bank's savings accounts, and are among the safest type of fund investments. While the value of your money-market mutual fund can decline, it is not common. In fall 2008, for example, a few money-market mutual funds did lose value.

Index funds are another type of stock fund that you need to know about. Index funds are typically managed by electronic software that selects stocks from a market index such as the Dow Jones Industrial Average or the S&P 500. The objective of these selections is to match the overall performance of the underlying index, which means that these funds are unlikely to do better or worse than the overall market index they are trying to mirror. If you have a 401K, it may well offer an index fund as one of its investment vehicles. Many mutual fund companies sell index funds.

Before you invest in a mutual fund, you should ask for the fund's prospectus, which is a booklet that gives you lots of valuable information about the fund's goals, strategies, principles, fees and expenses, and performance history. The prospectus will include some terms you may not be familiar with. Here are some of the more important ones:

- **Fund manager** The person or team responsible for managing the fund's holdings.

- **Load funds** Mutual funds that pay commissions to brokers.

- **No-load funds** Mutual funds with no commissions.

- **NTF (No Transaction Fee)** Mutual funds that can be bought in brokerage accounts without incurring transaction fees.

- **Expense ratio** The percent of the investor's money that the fund's management uses each year to run the fund. Typical expense ratios are between 1 and 1.5 percent.

- **International funds** Mutual funds whose underlying holdings are in foreign investments.

- **Balanced funds** Mutual funds whose underlying investments are a blend of stocks and bonds.

- ◆ **Sector funds** Funds that buy only companies in a specific industry, such as technology or health care.

- ◆ **Target funds** Also known as lifecycle funds or target maturity funds, these funds are targeted and managed for maximum benefit at a specific time period in the future, such as retirement.

- ◆ **Trailing performance** This term refers to the past returns or losses of the fund on an annual basis. Returns would include any yield such as dividends or interest paid from the underlying fund holdings plus or minus any appreciation or depreciation from those holdings.

When you're ready to take the plunge, pull out the prospectus for each of the funds you're considering, and use them to answer the questions in the Mutual Fund Comparison Guide. You can use this worksheet to compare the profiles and performance of as many as four funds.

> **In the Know**
>
> A prospectus makes for pretty dry reading. As an alternative, there are several companies and websites that publish some of the fund data you'll need to properly evaluate your mutual fund choices. Morningstar.com is one of the most popular.

Investing in Variable Annuities

Variable annuities are typically used as retirement investments, but unlike IRAs, the money you sock into a variable annuity isn't tax deductible. That's because variable annuities are considered to be insurance products. That insurance designation also means that there's no limit to the amount of money you can put into variable annuities, and you aren't forced to draw out of them at any specific age—two factors that also differentiate variable annuities from IRAs. Even though your earnings can compound tax-free within a variable annuity, when you withdraw your money, you'll be taxed at your normal tax rate on it, not at the typical capital gains rate for other investments like stocks or mutual funds.

def•i•ni•tion

> **Variable annuities** are insurance contracts in which the holder can select from a wide array of separate or sub accounts that mirror performance of a mutual fund.

Mutual Fund Comparison Guide

		Fund 1	Fund 2	Fund 3	Fund 4
	Fund Name	Big Company Stock Fund			
	Fund Ticker Symbol	xxxxx			
	Load or No-Load	No-load			
	Internal Expenses	0.9%			
	Turnover Ratio	75%			
	Manager Tenure	8 years			
	Percent U.S. Stocks	74%			
	Percent Non-U.S. Stocks	10%			
Sector Weightings (%):					
	Software	1%			
	Hardware	7%			
	Media	5%			
	Telcom	7%			
	Health Care	12%			
	Consumer Services	18%			
	Business Services	10%			
	Financial	5%			
	Consumer Goods	15%			
	Materials	8%			
	Energy	10%			
	Utilities	2%			
	Percent Bonds	12%			
	Average Credit Quality of Bonds	AA			
	Average Bond Maturity	4.25			
	Percent Cash	0.04			
	Inception Date of Fund	Feb-92			
	Price Earnings Ratio of Fund	12.1			
	Standard Deviation	12.2			
	Alpha	1.72			
	Beta	0.84			
Trailing Performance:					
	3 Month	-12.2%			
	1 Year	-14.4%			
	3 Years	2.5%			
	5 Years	5.6%			
	10 Years	9.8%			

The appeal of variable annuities used to be that tax deferral, but the low capital gains rate under current internal revenue code for sales of investments held for one year or longer blunts that advantage. Today, the appeal of variable annuities lies in their living benefits, which create a "floor" under your holdings with certain guarantees against risk of loss. There are many variations of these living benefits, and you would need to check with a professional advisor to see what variation may suit you best.

Variable annuities are commonly dismissed by the popular press as a bad investment choice, but I don't think we should tar these investments with such a broad brush. Yes, they have higher fees—in some cases substantially higher. But many investors who owned variable annuities during the huge market downturn in 2008 were quite happy to have paid the extra fees in order to build a floor under their market losses.

I won't dwell long on the topic of annuities, because they have limited appeal for most young or early stage investors. But at some stage, if you reach a point where you're looking for a retirement investment that goes beyond your 401K and IRAs, you might hear a sales pitch for variable annuities. If that happens, you'll be glad to at least understand how annuities work and whether they might work for you.

Variable annuities come with some drawbacks, or at least conditions, you should be aware of:

- **Death benefit:** Yes, most variable annuities offer a death benefit that guarantees that your beneficiaries will get back your investment, should you die before withdrawing your funds. That's the standard death benefit. If you want your beneficiaries to gain any interest or other yield from your investment, you'll have to buy an optional death benefit. I have seen many widows or widowers thrilled to know that their original investment gets returned to them when the overall value of the account has dropped since the original investment.

- **Surrender period and fines:** Most variable annuities fine you if you withdraw funds during a specified waiting period, called the surrender period—which can range from 0 to 10 years. The fines may start at 7 percent the first year, 6 percent the second, and so on. As you can see, these fines can be stiff, so this isn't a good place to put cash that you might need soon.

- **Early withdrawal fines:** Should you withdraw cash from a variable annuity before you reach age 59½, you can expect to pay an early withdrawal tax penalty of 10 percent—as is the case with other retirement savings plans.

- **Management and other fees:** Variable annuities come with a list of fees and expenses attached. The M&E (mortality and expense) fee is the charge associated with the insurance portion of your investment and its contract. These companies also may charge administrative expenses, operating expenses, and miscellaneous expenses. These charges will all be outlined in the variable annuity's prospectus.

When choosing a variable annuity, you'll want to compare these conditions, along with other fees, ratings (variable annuities are rated by Moody's, S&P, and others), the number of investment managers you'll have available to you, and so on. Variable annuities—sold by insurance companies and brokers—also provide a prospectus that should outline all of the terms, conditions, and charges. With those documents in hand, you can use the Variable Annuity Comparison worksheet to compare the offerings of up to three companies.

Features	Insurance Company ABC	Variable Annuity 2	Variable Annuity 3
Minimum Purchase Amount for IRAs	$2,000		
Minimum Purchase Amount for non-IRAs	$10,000		
Issue Ages	0-85		
Surrender Period	4 Years		
Surrender Schedule	7-6-5-4-0		
Investment Options	44		
Standard Death Benefit	Return of Premium +		
Optional Death Benefit	Yes		
Allocation Models Available	Yes		
A.M. Best Rating	A+		
Moody's Rating	Aa3		
S&P Rating	AA-		
Investment Managers	4		
Other Features			
M&E Expenses	1.50%		
Administrative Expenses	0.20%		
Miscellaneous Expenses	$30<$50K		
Subaccount Operating Expenses	Avg 1%		
Total Expenses	2.97%		

The Least You Need to Know

- If you decide to buy individual stocks, be prepared to educate yourself on the companies and stock offerings you're interested in. And look first to stocks within industries you have some familiarity with.

- Buying a bond is like loaning money to a company or a city/state/federal government, which then pays you back your initial investment and a set interest rate. Buying U.S. Treasury bonds is one of the simplest—and safest—ways to invest in individual bonds.

◆ Mutual funds are a simple and savvy way to build a diversified portfolio that is managed by a team of investment pros. Mutual funds can include stocks, bonds, and other securities, and they're the backbone of most 401K programs.

◆ Variable annuities are popular as retirement minded investments, but these retirement savings vehicles come with a unique set of benefits and a lot of fees, fines, and conditions, so read up on them carefully before investing.

11

Evaluating Your Current Investments

In This Chapter

- ◆ Finding out where your money is invested (and why it's invested there)
- ◆ How's that investment method working for you?
- ◆ Learning when to say "sell"!
- ◆ Keeping a lid on investment taxes

Whether you trade in stocks on a daily basis or toss your unopened 401K statements in a junk drawer, chances are good that right now some investments of some sort are lurking out there under your name. Like pets, if you have investments you need to take care of them. Unlike pets, however, if you take good care of your investments, they may take care of you one day (and, okay, I understand that your border collie takes out the garbage and does shiatsu, but he's not like other people's pets).

Step one in tending your litter of investments is to lay them out in front of you and evaluate what they represent, how you came to have them in the first place, and how well they're performing. And all of this evaluation needs to be unemotional, cool, objective, and honest. That's because investments are all about one thing, and one thing only—making money. The worksheets, charts, and lists in this chapter will help you evaluate your current investments *and* develop a more careful and objective way of knowing when to hold them and when to cash them out and move on. One final treat offered up by this chapter is a quick guide to determining the tax friendliness of your investments, so taxes won't take too big a bite from your holdings.

Determining What Kind of Investment Assets You Have

If you are invested in a 401K, you might think of that account as your investment. But, really, a 401K is to investment as a wallet is to money. The 401K holds the investments, but the actual investments are a collection of varied (as in diversified) assets. So, knowing that you have a 401K isn't the same as knowing what kind of investments you hold. In this section of the chapter, we're going to take a broad look at your investments, to determine just what kind of assets they represent.

It's All About Assets

You might have a variety of investment assets—a well-stocked money-market account, CDs, rental property, a small business you've started or invested in, some stocks you inherited, or the savings bonds your sainted grandmother has given you for your birthday every year. To evaluate your assets, you first have to identify all of them.

To begin to understand how your investments are allocated among all of these asset classes, go wa-a-a-y back to that Net Worth Calculator you put together back in Chapter 1. There, you listed all of your investment holdings—your savings accounts, investment accounts, life insurance, IRAs and other retirement accounts, real estate, business holdings, and so on. You can use the information from that Calculator (along with any supplemental account information you've gathered) to review your major investment asset holdings. You can also use the worksheets shown here—the Mutual Fund Summary, Stock Summary, Bond Summary, and Variable Annuity Summary—to note detailed information about these specific types of assets. (Check your 401K statement for specific information about what your account holds.)

Mutual Fund Summary

Mutual Fund	Broker / Custodian	Acct. No.	Retirement Account	Owner	Balance
Mutual Fund XYZ	Joe's Discount Broker	abcdef	Yes	BG	$ 1,930
U.S. Stock Fund	World's Biggest Broker	123456	No	BG	3,010
International Bond Fund	Mutual Fund Company QRS	ZYXWVU	No	Joint	7,752
Total Investment Accounts					$ 12,692

Stock Summary

Company	Broker / Custodian	Acct. No.	Retirement Account	Owner	# of Shares	Price per Share	Balance
Large Manufacturing Company	Joe's Discount Broker	abcdef	Yes	BG	50	$ 14.25	$ 713
Small Widget Maker	World's Biggest Broker	123456	No	BG	75	$ 16.18	1,214
International Widgets	Full-Service Broker	ZYXWVU	No	Joint	20	$ 22.65	453
Total Stock Positions							$ 2,380

Bond Summary

Company	Broker / Custodian	Acct. No.	Retirement Account	Owner	Maturity Date	Coupon Rate	Current Market Value
Large Conglomerate	World's Smallest Broker	abcdef	Yes	BG	03/27/11	5.00%	$ 1,725
Small Widget Maker	World's Biggest Broker	123456	No	BG	12/09/12	4.50%	2,874
International Widgets	Full-Service Broker	ZYXWVU	No	Joint	04/09/14	6.00%	4,516
Total Bond Positions							$ 9,115

Variable Annuity Summary

Variable Annuity Name	Insurance Company / Custodian	Acct. No.	Retirement Account	Owner	Beneficiary	Balance
Retirement Spectrum	Insurance Company ABC	abcdef	No	Joint	Kids	$ 4,726
Personal Pension	Variable Annuity Company 123	123456	Yes	BG	MG	7,845
New Annuity	Big Insurance Company	ZYXWVU	Yes	Joint	Charity	6,492
Total Variable Annuity Positions						$ 19,063

Assessing Your Allocations

Okay, you now have a very clear picture of all your investment holdings. Now, it's time to determine what kind of assets they represent. The first step in that process is to understand that assets fall into a distinct set of classes. I've talked about all of these asset classes, but let's review:

- **Cash** assets include money you have at hand (of course) as well as cash you can get to in less than 30 days, such as bank accounts, money markets, and short-term U.S. Treasury Bills.

- **Stocks,** as you learned in the previous chapter of this book, are equity holdings or shares of publicly owned companies.

- **Bonds** represent debt that you hold from companies, governments, or government agencies.

- **Real estate** assets are land or buildings in which you have an ownership stake.

- **Commodities** are material goods, such as gold, silver, lumber, cotton, and so on, as well as shares you hold in funds, partnerships, and trusts that hold these materials as investments.

- **Life insurance products** are an asset group that includes *fixed annuities* and life insurance policies.

def•i•ni•tion

Fixed annuities are those that offer a set interest rate and the potential for a series of equal payouts over a fixed period of time. (Compare these with variable annuities, which you learned about in Chapter 10.)

As a wise investor, you want to determine how well the assets you hold match these three criteria:

- The time frame you have for investing (how long you intend to hold the investment)

- Your risk tolerance (remember that Risk Tolerance Questionnaire you completed back in Chapter 9?)

- Your investment needs (are you looking to save for retirement or your kids' education, or do you need to get some supplemental income asap?)

If you want your investment portfolio to meet all of these criteria, it must be balanced. That means it must contain the right mix of assets to meet your investment needs (I'll talk more about maintaining a strong investment portfolio and rebalancing your assets in Chapter 12; for now, we're just getting a broad overview of your holdings). So, for example, if having plenty of quick cash available to you is more important right now than pulling in maximum investment earnings, you might have put a good portion of your investment dollars in money markets, Treasury Bills, or CDs. If, on the other hand, you have enough ready money and you're more interested in scoring some strong dividends, your portfolio might hold a larger portion of growth stocks. If you simply can't afford to lose a penny, your portfolio might hold a high portion of safer, short-term bonds, fixed annuities, and cash equivalents.

Take a look at all of your holdings, and then use the Asset Allocation Checklist to determine the overall allocations of your current investments.

Asset Allocation Checklist

My assets include:

- ☐   Cash
- ☐   Stocks
- ☐   Bonds
- ☐   Real Estate
- ☐   Commodities
- ☐   Private Company Ownership
- ☐   My portfolio is well diversified

My allocation matches my:

- ☐   Time Frame
- ☐   Risk Tolerance
- ☐   Investment Needs

My allocation is rebalanced (by me or by a fund manager):

- ☐   As needed
- ☐   On an automatic basis in scheduled intervals
  - ☐   Monthly
  - ☐   Quarterly
  - ☐   Annually

How Well Is Your Investment Method Working?

If I were to ask you why and how you'd chosen all of the assets you've just been reviewing, could you tell me? I'm not talking about the commercial building you inherited or those savings bonds you received as birthday presents. I mean, what method do you use to choose the investments you have? Do you make monthly contributions to a mutual fund that you chose based on its asset classes? Do you buy a CD from your local bank every 90 days, as a matter of habit? Are you buying individual stocks in entertainment companies every six months because you spend a lot of time at the movies and have a good sense of which companies are hot in the industry? Or did you simply check the first box in your 401K signup sheet and now allow your monthly contributions to trickle into whatever fund that box represented?

If you haven't adopted a method for making investments, you should. That method should include contingencies for investing in all of the asset classes you hold (or intend to hold), and all of your choices should be in keeping with a big picture view of your investment goals. If you have a history of making individual and sometimes off-the-cuff decisions about your investments, now is the time to rewrite history. Determine how and why you want to invest, and then use those guidelines when making your choices.

In the Know

When you're assessing the performance of your portfolio, don't forget about our good friends at Morningstar.com. You can go to that website and do a search to get performance histories for your stocks and mutual funds.

No matter what method you're using, you need to make sure that it's working for you. In other words, you need to follow—closely—the performance of your investments. You'll receive an annual report from all of your mutual funds, and you'll get monthly statements on the performance of your IRAs and other investment accounts. Tracking the value of real estate holdings can be a bit trickier, although you can certainly keep an eye on real estate values for similar properties in the area.

Setting a Sell Discipline

Another important factor in your investment method is setting a specific threshold for when you will sell the investments you're holding. Some investors are highly disciplined about selling. They might, for example, determine that they're going to sell any stock when it reaches 75 percent of its historic high value, or they will sell any stock that falls below 80 percent of its normal value. In other words, they set a target price for selling, and they stick to it.

Unfortunately, a lot of casual investors don't live by a sound sell discipline. They hang onto those bonds because they were a gift, or they buy that CD because they've always bought that CD. You don't want to be one of these investors. Remember what I said earlier: you're invested in *anything* because you want to make money. If an investment you're holding isn't performing up to your standards, then be prepared to sell it and move on.

First, of course, you have to set those standards—or devise your own sell discipline. To begin, simply look at the underlying fundamentals of each of your investments. If any of them doesn't hit the three criteria we talked about earlier (time frame, risk tolerance, needs), they don't belong in your portfolio. Now, consider each investment's performance. If you had new cash to invest, would you invest it in this vehicle today? If so, you're probably going to hold on to it for a while. If not, it might be a good candidate for selling off. The Investment Sell Discipline Checklist will help you consider some of the criteria that might go into your decision.

Investment Sell Discipline Checklist

☐ The stock or fund has reached its target price and there is no evidence that your target price should be higher.

☐ The money could be invested elsewhere, in a different asset that you would rather own.

☐ There are other investments that you would like to buy or should buy to achieve your balanced asset allocation.

☐ The stock's fundamental strengths or financial situation have deteriorated or the market within which the company operates is weakening substantially.

☐ The holding has become too large a percentage of your overall portfolio.

☐ The fund has had a significant manager change and you are not able to evaluate the new manager's abilities.

☐ The company's earnings and sales are slowing down.

☐ Your original purchase decision was flawed.

☐ The stock has become overvalued.

☐ There has been significant negative news about the stock, fund, or bond you're holding.

☐ The company is encountering stiff new competition.

☐ Your reason for buying no longer exists.

You'll develop your sell discipline over time, as you spend more time analyzing your investments and tracking their performance. But always remember that selling is just as important as buying when it comes to forming your investment method and allocating your assets.

Pitfall Alert! _____

Don't allow sentiment or emotion to guide your investment choices. Just because your Uncle Leo works for Acme Salami and Rat Control, Inc., you shouldn't feel compelled to buy stock in the company. Remember: investing is all about money, money, money. Choose investments objectively and wisely.

Are Your Investments Tax-Friendly?

One final aspect of your investments worth noting is their tax efficiency. Sorry, but I don't recommend that you sit back and coast when it comes to monitoring the taxability of your investment choices. Some investments, particularly those that produce high yields, interest, or dividends, will add to your tax burden. And some mutual fund managers are constantly buying and selling stocks within their funds, which triggers short-term gains, for which you *will* be taxed.

If you are absolutely committed to paying the least amount of taxes possible, you need to consider the impact of your investments on your tax burden. If you're extremely conservative, for example, you might consider money-market funds to be poor investments because all of those holdings are taxable. On the other hand, maybe you care more about the yield of your investments than you do about the amount of tax you have to pay on them. In any event, you can determine the tax efficiency of most investments by asking three simple questions. For each investment that you hold, use the following Tax Efficiency Checklist to ask yourself three short questions. If you have more than one checkmark on this form, you probably need to reconsider your holdings.

Tax Efficiency Checklist

☐ Does your investment have a high taxable yield from interest or dividends?

☐ Does your mutual fund turn over the underlying holdings more frequently than annually?

☐ Does your fund manager routinely harvest losses to offset gains?

The Least You Need to Know

- ◆ To evaluate your investment holdings, first determine what types of assets your investments represent and how well those assets match your investment goals, objectives, and needs.

- ◆ Your criteria for buying investments should work toward creating a portfolio that fits the 'big picture' of your investment plan. A haphazard approach to investing won't give you strong results.

- ◆ Develop and stick with a sell discipline that sets target prices or other specific criteria for selling any investment. That way, you can reinvest the money in something that makes a better fit in your portfolio.

- ◆ If taxes are an important issue for you, don't forget to monitor the taxability of your investment yields, dividends, or interest.

Chapter 12

Maintaining a Winning Investment Strategy

In This Chapter

◆ Keeping your portfolio on an even keel

◆ Maintaining an eye on mutual fund performance

◆ Assessing the ups and downs of bond values

◆ Exploring alternative investments

You have a lot of tools at your disposal for choosing the investments that fill your portfolio. That's the first part of your responsibility as an investor. In fact, you can think of your investments as seeds you've planted in the rich, loamy garden of the marketplace (or, in the hard, arid desert of the marketplace, whichever metaphor seems more appropriate on any given day). Your second task is to keep a watchful eye on the "garden" in your portfolio, to ensure that it's continuing to produce. If investments fail to thrive, you may need to yank them out and try again. At the same time, successful investments that have given you the output you were expecting from them might be better replaced with fresh seedling investments.

In short, you have to monitor how your investments are faring and make strategic decisions about which investments to hold and which to sell. The worksheets in this chapter will help you manage those tasks. From monitoring your asset allocations to assessing the performance of your mutual funds and comparing the costs and benefits of alternative investment holdings, the tools in this chapter will help make the work of maintaining your investment strategy an easier row to hoe.

Asset Allocation and Rebalancing

One of the surest ways to get the most from your investment portfolio is to make certain that it contains assets that are most likely to meet your savings goals and objectives. Most investment values vary over time, growing and diminishing in response to shifting global and market forces. Your job is to keep your portfolio on track by monitoring those value changes and adjusting your investments accordingly.

I've talked about a number of different types of investments throughout this book, and by now you've probably realized that one person's idea of a balanced portfolio might differ substantially from someone else's interpretation of that term. I can't tell you what kind of assets your portfolio should hold, but I can show you how various types of assets stack up in terms of risks and rewards.

As you can see in the Investment Pyramid, assets such as traditional checking and savings accounts, money-market accounts, savings bonds, and so on, are typically considered to be lower risk investments, and historically, they have tended to offer lower returns than other asset types. Moving up through the pyramid, you find assets that involve increasing risks that come with the *potential* for higher returns. You can use this pyramid as a general guide when determining what types of investments might fit best with your own risk tolerance and investment performance desires.

In Chapter 11, you pulled together summaries of your asset holdings—mutual funds, stocks, bonds, and annuities—to get a general idea of your portfolio holdings. You also carefully considered why and how you chose the assets that fill your portfolio. You're even working on your own investment method and sell discipline—right? Now it's time to draw a more detailed picture of your assets, so you can determine whether they accurately reflect your investment method and goals.

Use the Asset Allocation and Rebalancing worksheet to list all of the assets currently in your portfolio and their current values. The worksheet will tally the subtotal of each asset class and the percentage of your total holdings that class represents. Next, fill in the percentage of your holdings you *want* that asset class to represent. The worksheet will then show you how much of an adjustment (through sales and/or added investment) you need to make to bring your portfolio into balance with those goals.

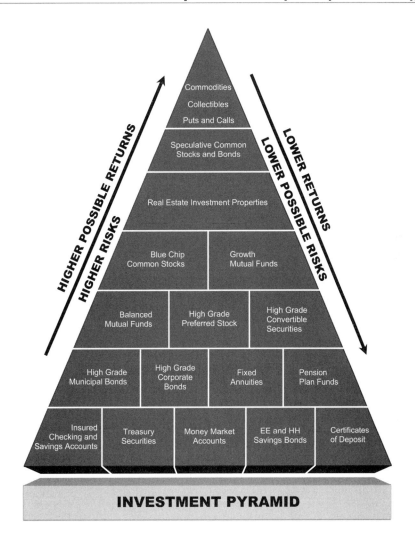

INVESTMENT PYRAMID

Many investors set a variance limit for how much they are willing to allow an asset class to increase or decrease in terms of its percentage of their total portfolio value. When any class of holdings changes beyond that limit, it's time to rebalance. So, let's say that you've decided that you want to maintain 10 percent of your portfolio in stocks, and you're only willing to allow a 10 percent increase or decrease from that goal. If your stock holdings ramp up to 12 percent of your total portfolio, they've increased by 20 percent. At that point, you may want to think about selling some of those stocks and using the money to bump up other areas of your portfolio to reach your desired allocation.

	A	B	C
1	**Asset Allocation and Rebalancing**		
2		**Asset Class**	**Investment Description**
3			
4		**Cash**	Bank Account 1
5			Bank Account 2
6			CD 1
7			CD 2
8			U.S. Savings Bond
9		**Subtotal Cash**	
10			
11		**Bonds**	XYZ Bond Fund
12			City of Boston Bond
13			U.S. Treasury Note
14			The Hi Yield Bond Fund
15		**Subtotal Bonds**	
16			
17		**Stocks**	100 Shares XYZ
18			The Growth Fund of Nappy
19			The Julia Value Fund
20			17 Shares of My Employer
21		**Subtotal Stocks**	
22			
23		**Investment Real Estate**	123 Main Street
24			New Hampshire Condo
25			The JNAP REIT
26		**Subtotal Investment Real Estate**	
27			
28		**Private Company Ownership**	My Company
29			My Neighbors Company
30			The Croner Store
31		**Subtotal Private Company Ownership**	
32			
33		**Commodities**	The Joan Natural Resources Fund
34			1 Ounce Gold
35			The Timberland REIT
36			Oil ETF
37			
38		**Subtotal Commodities**	
39			
40			
41		**Totals**	

	D	E	F	G	H
1					
2	Investment Value	Percent of Total Portfolio	Asset Class Total Percentage	Desired Asset Class Total Percentage	Adjustment Required
3					
4	1,000	1%			
5	-	0%			
6	5,000	6%			
7	-	0%			
8	2,500	3%			
9	8,500		10%	5%	-5%
10					
11	2,000	2%			
12	100	0%			
13	1,500	2%			
14	1,000	1%			
15	4,600		6%	20%	14%
16					
17	7,000	8%			
18	1,500	2%			
19	1,200	1%			
20	900	1%			
21	10,600		13%	55%	42%
22					
23	10,000	12%			
24	15,000	18%			
25	2,000	2%			
26	27,000		33%	10%	-23%
27					
28	25,000	30%			
29	1,000	1%			
30	500	1%			
31	26,500		32%	5%	-27%
32					
33	1,500	2%			
34	200	0%			
35	2,500	3%			
36	1,400	2%			
37					
38	5,600		7%	5%	-2%
39					
40					
41	$ 82,800			100%	

In the Know _____

How often you rebalance your portfolio is up to you. Some people do it on a regular basis—every month, every quarter, every six months, or maybe just once a year. Other folks check their portfolio frequently and rebalance whenever any asset class moves out of the percentage range they've set for it.

Monitoring the Performance of Your Mutual Funds

Even though mutual funds are managed by a team of professional financial researchers and investment analysts, you can't just throw money at them and assume all will be well. Nope, you still have to keep tabs on how your mutual fund investments are faring in the marketplace.

def•i•ni•tion _____

Trailing performance refers to the past returns or losses of a fund, as calculated on an annual basis.

Now, I'm not talking about comparing the performance of your corporate bond fund to the performance of a large U.S. or foreign stock fund. But you *do* need to compare how your mutual fund is performing against other similar funds in the marketplace. To do that, you can consider its *trailing performance* in comparison to the trailing performance of other funds in similar categories.

The Mutual Fund Performance worksheet offers a quick method for comparing the performance of four different mutual funds against the S&P 500 stock index, the Dow Jones Industrial Average, Lehman Brothers Aggregate Bond index (currently owned and maintained by Barclays Capital), and the MSCI EAFE index (that's the Morgan Stanley Capital International index of stocks from Europe, Australia, and the Far East—okay, you can wake up now). If you see that your mutual fund is lagging far behind the relevant index indicators, you can begin considering whether you should move your investment into another, better performing fund. There is an index for just about every major market in the world, so pick the index that most closely represents the holdings you are trying to mimic and have at it.

The Mutual Fund Comparison Guide from Chapter 10 is a very helpful tool for choosing a mutual fund for investment. You can use that guide to compare the performance of four funds.

	A	B	C	D	E	F	G
1	**Mutual Fund Performance**						
2		**Trailing Performance**		Fund 1	Fund 2	Fund 3	Fund 4
3							
4		3 Months					
5		12 Months					
6		1 Year					
7		3 Years					
8		5 Years					
9		10 Years					
10							
11							
12		**Index Trailing Performance**					
13							
14		**S&P 500**					
15							
16		3 Months					
17		12 Months					
18		1 Year					
19		3 Years					
20		5 Years					
21		10 Years					
22							
23		**Dow Jones Industrial Average**					
24							
25							
26		**Lehman Brothers Aggregate Bond Index**					
27		3 Months					
28		12 Months					
29		1 Year					
30		3 Years					
31		5 Years					
32		10 Years					
33							
34		**MSCI EAFE Index**					
35							
36		3 Months					
37		12 Months					
38		1 Year					
39		3 Years					
40		5 Years					
41		10 Years					
42							

To find the latest information on the performance of just about any mutual fund, you can order a prospectus, or take the more efficient route of checking the performance online. There are numerous sites that offer fund performance results, but www. morningstar.com has an easy-to-use search tool and easy-to-read results.

> **In the Know** _____
>
> Mutual fund management comes in two varieties—active and passive. Active management means that the fund manager is continually assessing the marketplace to determine what areas of the market will be the most advantageous for investment. Passive managers just invest in an index, fill their baskets with a bit of everything, and let it ride. Either approach has merits. And, you might change the style you seek in a fund manager—over time, as you become more familiar with the markets and the process of investing. Most online market monitoring sites also provide information about fund managers, so you can check into the performance history of the management of any fund you hold or are considering buying into.

Comparing Bond Values and Interest Rates

I don't have much in the way of a fast, quick, easy method for tracking the performance of your bonds. Nevertheless, it's important that you understand how to assess how well your investment in bonds is performing. To evaluate a bond's performance, you have to consider both the bond's value and its interest rate. When interest rates rise, bond value decreases; lower interest rates result in higher bond value. That means that part of a bond's risk is attached to fluctuating market interest rates. Let me explain how that works.

> **Pitfall Alert!** _____
>
> If you think you may have to sell a bond before it matures, you *really* need to keep track of interest rate changes in the marketplace to avoid losing money when you sell. This warning doesn't apply, of course, when you intend to hold a bond until it matures.

Let's say that last year you bought a $10,000 bond with a 10-year maturity period that pays a 5 percent interest rate. Over the course of a year, that bond pays you $500 in interest. Today, the interest rate on a similar bond has shot up to 6 percent. At this point, you might feel compelled to sell the bond, but how do you do that? Who wants the low-ball interest rate on your 5 percent bond when you can purchase a similar one at 6 percent? At 6 percent interest, the new bond would pay $600 per year in interest. To move that baby you'll have to sell it at a discounted price—$9,300 might bring it into line with a $10,000 bond at the going interest rate of 6 percent. On the other hand, what if you bought the bond at 6 percent and now that similar bond pays 5 percent? Maybe you want to sell it to take advantage of your position. If so, you might ask $10,700 for your bond, to account for its higher interest rate.

Again, online investment research sites such as zacks.com, schaeffer.com, and the oft-mentioned (at least by me) Morningstar.com track bond fund performance, so you'll always have access to fast facts about your bonds' current condition. But now that you know how bond performance is assessed, you'll have a much better idea what those performance indicators mean.

Making Alternative Investments

Okay, you might be wondering, just what *is* an alternative investment? If you make alternative investments, do you have to wear hemp, believe in aliens, or attend the Burning Man festival with your stockbroker? Or do alternative investments make you edgy, urban, and alive? Well, no. An alternative investment is simply an investment in something other than stocks and bonds. And, as you've read previously in this book, there are a lot of alternatives when it comes to investing. These alternatives include, for example, *hedge funds*, venture capital, real estate, and gold, silver, and other commodities—things that will eventually be converted into liquid assets.

The reason that alternative investments receive so much attention (and they do, in the financial world), is that some major investors—most specifically, those who manage the endowments for Ivy League universities such as Yale and Harvard—have done very, very well with them. These universities might hold 30 percent to 40 percent of their portfolios in alternative investments.

def•i•ni•tion

Hedge funds are pools of money that are exempt from most of the rules and regulations that govern most other mutual funds. They typically use a lot of aggressive strategies to accomplish their aggressive investing goals. These are 'big fish' funds, with minimums ranging from $250,000 to $1,000,000 or more, in many cases, and carry a number of investor restrictions.

But you need to be aware that you probably can't do as well as these Ivy League players in the alternative investment arena. Why? First, because these endowments are drawing upon the expertise of some of the top investment analysts in the country—maybe in the world, for that matter. Also, they can invest huge sums of money, and then let that money ride for a long time. In addition to offering less liquidity, alternative investments require these longer time commitments in order to pay off.

It's hard for the little guy to make good in alternative investments, but if you're considering giving it a try, I encourage you to use the Alternative Investment Comparison worksheet to review your options. You can use this form to compare the restrictions, qualifications, yields, and return objectives of up to five alternatives you might be considering. Remember, even these alternative investment choices must fit with your overall investment goals, so tally up the facts and consider them carefully in relation to those goals when making your decision.

Alternative Investment Comparison

	Alternative Choice 1	Alternative Choice 2	Alternative Choice 3	Alternative Choice 4	Alternative Choice 5
Alternative Investment Name	Rob's R.E. Partners				
Minimum Investment	$5,000				
Liquidity Provisions	none				
Investor Qualification Criteria	5-year minimum investment period				
Yield	4%				
Level of Risk	medium				
Estimated Holding Period	10 years				
Total Return Objective (%)	12%				

The Least You Need to Know

◆ The assets within your investment portfolio should reflect your investment goals and strategies. To maintain the right balance, determine what percentage of the total value of your holdings should come from each asset class, then adjust your holdings periodically to maintain that balance.

◆ You can monitor the performance of your mutual funds by comparing it against similar funds and the leading market indexes such as the S&P 500, the Dow Jones Industrial Average, and so on.

◆ Bond values go up when market rates of interest go down, and bond values go down when market rates of interest rise. If you intend to sell a bond before its maturity date, you need to follow market rate changes carefully to avoid losing money when you sell.

◆ Alternative investments have been very successful for some large institutions, but you shouldn't count on repeating their success. If you're a beginner, you need to tread slowly and carefully with these investments.

Part 4

Planning for the Future

Savings and investment are an important part of planning for the future, but you also have to have a working plan for specific *parts* of that future. The tools in Chapters 13 through 16 are here to help!

Need a plan for paying for your education? Or are you planning ahead for your kids' college days? Either way, we have some tools that will make your planning easier. Maybe you're focused on your retirement. If so, we have some worksheets for that process, too, from calculating the cost of living your own version of the good life, to setting up the accounts you'll need to make it happen. We even make thinking about the unthinkable a bit more bearable, by helping you manage some essential estate-planning tasks.

Of course, we realize that at some point you might reach limits of your 'do-it-yourself' interests and skills. For those times, we offer some tools and guidelines for choosing, working with, and evaluating financial professionals. That way, you can continue to make good decisions about your finances, even when you've called in outside help.

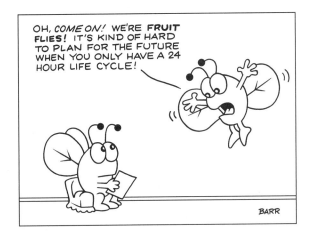

Chapter 13

Education Planning

In This Chapter

- ◆ Making a smart college-savings plan
- ◆ What kinds of funds will you need?
- ◆ Analyzing your options

Saving up for a college education is serious business, but it's also easy to neglect. In good times, it's tempting to sock your savings into securities that offer the allure of high returns. In bad times, it can be difficult to devote your dwindling resources to a college fund. "My kid's bright," you tell yourself. "She'll get all the financial aid she needs." Unfortunately, during hard economic times, grants, scholarships, and funds for student loans dry up, and who knows when hard times are just around the corner. That's why you need to be at least *thinking* about how you'll handle future educational costs.

This chapter gives you some important tools for the task of planning for those costs. These worksheets will help you get your arms around exactly what kind of education you might be planning to finance, how much that education might cost, and *all* of your options for meeting those costs. In the end, you may determine that other savings needs trump education in your current financial playing field. But you'd be a dunce not to at least stop and put a little bit of time and thought into making that determination now—before your teen starts bringing home college recruitment brochures.

Thinking Through Your Plan

What's the smartest way to save for future educational costs? The answer really depends on what you're saving for. If you are committed to sending your child to the private liberal arts school of his or her dreams, your saving strategy might be very different than if you are fully on-board with funding a community college education, but expect your son or daughter to take on educational expenses above and beyond that goal. Or maybe you intend to do a little of both.

We'll get into the specifics of determining your future costs in the next section, but for now, let's focus on the broad picture. According to the College Board, average tuition and fees for a private, four-year college for the 2007–2008 academic year were nearly $24,000—up more than 6 percent from the previous year. That compares to the nearly $6,200 costs for a public four-year school during that same year. Public two-year school costs for the 2007–2008 academic year averaged just under $2,400 dollars.

? In the Know _____

Remember that averages are just that. Every state and every institution has its own tuition/fees/costs profile. The average annual cost of attending a public school in Vermont, for example, is nearly twice that in Idaho. Go to allcollege.org to find a state-by-state breakdown of average costs for public and private educational institutions.

Remember, these are just tuition and fees. In 2006, the U.S. Department of Education estimated that year's total costs (tuition, fees, room and board) for a private four-year educational institution at $29,925, and the same costs for a public four-year school at $12,285. The Department of Education has calculated averages for every state; you can find them at www.allcollege.org.

Again, you want to get the big picture of your college-savings plan in focus right now. Consider these questions:

- What type of college education (public, private, four-year, two-year) do you realistically expect to help your child fund?

- How much of the costs of that education are you willing to bear?

- How much of the annual cost do you believe your child should be responsible for?

- How much of the cost will need to be absorbed by financial aid such as loans, grants, and scholarships?

- What conditions will you place on your continued participation in this plan? Will you demand that your child maintain a certain grade point average, or hold a part-time job during the academic year? Will you require your child to find a work-study program, or spend a specified amount of time after high school and before college, earning and saving?

After you've considered these questions, use the College Funding Organizer to record your answers and play with a variety of scenarios for multiple funding options. This worksheet helps you sketch out a framework for the savings task that lies before you.

	A	B	C	D
1	**College Funding Organizer**			
2		College Name	Expensive Private School	Your State School
3		Estimated Cost per Year	$45,000	$23,000
4		Funding from Parents	$20,000	$20,000
5		Funding from Student	$5,000	0
6		Funding from Scholarship	$3,000	$3,000
7		Funding from Loans	$10,000	
8		Funding from Grants	$7,000	
9		Criteria for Parent Participation	3.0 GPA or better	3.0 GPA or better
10		Other Criteria or Restrictions	Summer Work	Summer Work

If you're trying to decide how to pay for your *own* return for an advanced degree, don't forget that many employers will foot at least part of the bill for their employees' professional development. Talk to your boss or human resources point person to find out what tuition assistance is available to you.

Pitfall Alert!

Don't assume that a private, Ivy League education is your child's only answer for a top-drawer career. Many state schools—University of California at Berkeley or UC Santa Barbara are just two examples—have strong, highly regarded academic programs. When it comes time to choose, check placement stats and alumnae profiles to find state schools that excel in your child's chosen field.

Calculating How Much You Can Save

Projecting costs for your child's education isn't as difficult as it might seem. Several respected online sites have calculators that perform that task simply and with some accuracy (collegeboard.com and salliemae.com are just two of them). Determining how you're going to pony up the dough, however, takes a lot more time and thought.

You've already weighed the big choices—private versus public, four-year versus two-year. Now, choose some schools that fit your big-picture profile, and visit their sites to find their current annual tuitions, and their estimates of annual fees and room, board, and book costs (typically, tuition represents just under 40 percent of the total annual cost of a college education). With that information, you have an estimate of what it would cost for your child to attend these schools this year. Most sources estimate that education inflation clips along at 6 percent or 7 percent every year. That gives you a good idea of how the costs will rise before your young one heads off for freshman orientation.

With all of this information in mind, turn to the College Savings Planner to calculate the total future cost of your child's four-year education—which will appear on line 14 of the worksheet. Now, enter in the after-tax rate of return you're receiving on your current investments, or the rate you plan to shoot for in your college-savings fund. When you enter that percentage, the worksheet calculates the monthly savings you'll have to invest to hit that four-year cost.

	A	B	C
1	**College Savings Planner**		
2			
3			
4			
5	Current Annual Cost of College		$ 25,000
6	Number of Years Until First Year of College		14
7	Education Inflation Rate		6.00%
8			
9	Future Cost of 1st Year of College		$ 56,523
10	Future Cost of 2nd Year of College		$ 59,914
11	Future Cost of 3rd Year of College		$ 63,509
12	Future Cost of 4th Year of College		$ 67,319
13			
14	Total Future Cost of Four-Year College		$ 247,265
15			
16			
17	After-Tax Rate of Return on Investments		8.00%
18			
19	Monthly Savings Required *		$802.75
20			
21	Note: * Assumes savings completed by time child enters college		

Okay, you can stop laughing (or crying), now. Few folks can take on this much of an additional savings commitment in the early stages of their career (or even in midcareer, for that matter). In reality, the amount you sock away for your child's education will be constrained by your cash flow (you learned all about that back in Chapter 3). And, remember, this worksheet's monthly savings amount is what you'd need to save if you were to pay the entire cost of your child's education on your own. You can play with a number of scenarios here, based on your projections for grants, loans, scholarships, and other aid—so let's talk about that aid now.

Pitfall Alert!

Think carefully before cutting back on retirement savings to fund a college-savings plan. If you aren't able to live on your income after retirement, your child will have a lot more to worry about than why he or she had to go to State U. instead of Yale. Your college-funding plan isn't a good one if it jeopardizes your own financial future.

In the Know

Your child can do a lot to lighten the financial burden of his or her education by getting good grades, planning early for college admission and scholarship competitions, and by earning some of the money for his or her own education. Consider creative plans. Maybe your son or daughter could start out at a low-cost state or community college, then transfer after the first two years to a more desirable (and expensive) private or Ivy League school. Talk with parents who are grappling with college costs now to find out what they've learned about the process. Start researching scholarships early and treat the search like it's your job. Just don't hide your head in the sand!

Your Options: 529 Plans, Financial Aid, Grants, and Loans

Now that you know without question that you'll desperately need some kind of financial assistance in footing the bill for your child's higher education, let's talk more about what's available to you. (Acronym alert! The financial aid process triggers an alphabetic avalanche of not-so-catchy form and program monikers.)

Before any government or institution agrees to give you financial assistance for your child's college education, you will need to fill out a FAFSA (Free Application for Federal Student Aid). For a preview of the fun ahead, you can find these forms online at www.fafsa.ed.gov. After you've submitted the form, the feds will fill out yet another form in the name of your budding young student—a SAR, or Student Aid Report—that will be sent to the college your son or daughter has chosen to attend. That school will use the SAR to determine your financial need. It does that by calculating your EFC, or Expected Family Contribution, and subtracting that amount from the total projected cost of your child's education.

Every institution uses its own formula to calculate this EFC figure, as does the federal government. State schools and private schools typically have two totally different ways of funding scholarships, with the state school approach typically being the more liberal of those approaches. Many state schools, for example, don't count the equity you have in your home as an available asset for funding Junior's education. That private school may chuck that equity right into your EFC.

You can find an excellent general EFC calculator at collegeboard.com. Your financial situation may change dramatically between now and the time you're actually applying for this aid, but the calculator gives you a good look at the process you'll be working through.

That good old FAFSA will line you up for applying for a number of types of aid, including Pell Grants, and all federal, state, and institutional financial programs. Let's talk about some of the types of aid you can shoot for as supplements to your savings program.

In the Know

You'd be amazed at the number and variety of scholarships available to most students, based on their academic performance, family financial background, ethnicity, special interests, geographic roots, and numerous other qualifications. Your child's guidance counselor can help you explore these options, and you can find lots of information online at financialaidfinder.com and ed.gov/finaid.

First, let's look at some loan options:

- **Federal Stafford Student Loans (SSLs):** These federal government loans provide low fixed-interest rates (currently 6 percent) and are one of the cheapest ways to borrow money for college. They have tight eligibility requirements, so investigate them early to determine how well you qualify (www.staffordloan.com).

- **PLUS Loans for grads and parents:** These government loans also come with a fixed interest rate (8.5 percent in 2008) and will cover all of the costs of your child's education, minus available financial aid.

◆ **Private student loans:** Private lenders offer student loans of as much as $40,000 annually. These loans charge higher interest rates than do Stafford or PLUS loans, but might be worth exploring if those programs don't work for you. Most of these loans are deferred until after graduation, at which stage they require monthly payments, just like any other loan.

And loans aren't your only options. Consider these sources of financial aid:

◆ **529 savings plans:** 529 plans are offered by states or financial institutions to help families save for college. The plans typically are either savings plans with regular investment contributions, or prepaid plans in which you prepay expenses at a qualifying institution. 529 savings plans are similar to a 401K or IRA, in that your regular contributions are invested in mutual funds or other investment options of your choosing. Investment earnings are tax-deferred, and distributions that go directly to pay for college costs are federally tax-free. Many states also offer tax breaks for those who invest in these plans. You retain control of the funds, and can move them around every year. And, you can deposit as much as $300,000 per student in these funds. You can set these up through a 529 plan manager or a financial advisor (see www.savingforcollege.com for more).

◆ **Grants:** Federal Pell Grants pay a portion of college costs for students who qualify for this type of financial assistance. The amount of these grants is low right now (about $4,700) and can only be used at specific qualifying institutions. But, the grants need not be repaid (learn more about Pell Grants at www.studentaid.ed.gov).

◆ **Work-study options:** A number of colleges and universities offer work-study programs, in which students work part of the academic year to repay their educational costs.

◆ **Learn and serve grants:** Other programs enable students to work in community service programs for one or two years prior to beginning college, in order to earn money toward their college tuition, along with a monthly stipend for living costs. Some of these programs are international, giving your child an opportunity for an even broader educational experience. The Corporation for National and Community Service program is an example of a privately managed program that complements the Federal Work-Study program (learn more at www.learnandserve.gov). I strongly encourage you to consider the broad benefits available to young people who experience the responsibility and satisfaction of contributing meaningful service to their local, national, or international community—benefits that go well beyond the funding they'll receive toward their college tuition.

These aren't all of your options, of course. You can consider tapping into your home equity or your IRAs to help fund college costs, but remember that word of warning I offered on endangering your future to help pay for your child's education. One of the most important things you can do to fund your child's college education is to include a college-savings plan of any sort in your budget and to stick with it. Saving for anything, as you've learned throughout this book, requires discipline and a firm focus on the future. There's never a time when that kind of discipline is more necessary than when you're preparing to help secure your son or daughter's educational options.

If you're facing a college tuition hit soon, don't panic. Pick up some of the many detailed guides available for the application and financing process (see Appendix B for a couple of books to start you off). Then, use the College Aid, Grant, and Loan Checklist to ensure that you have your bases covered. Check off the items as you complete them, and keep your eyes firmly focused on the road ahead. Your student will thank you—maybe by scoring a high-paying job and chipping in on your retirement villa in Albuquerque.

College Aid, Grant, and Loan Checklist

I have:

☐ Performed extensive Internet searches to learn more about financial aid.

☐ Reviewed and completed a Free Application for Federal Student Aid (FAFSA).

☐ Completed any necessary college-specific financial aid applications.

☐ Submitted applications early.

☐ Followed application instructions carefully.

☐ Met with high school guidance counselors.

☐ Met with college financial aid officers.

☐ Gathered letters of recommendation.

☐ Been extremely courteous in my applications, remembering always to say "please" and "thank you."

☐ Followed up to be sure that my application was received and is complete.

☐ Started early and treated looking for scholarships as if it were my job.

☐ Researched all available scholarships, including local scholarships (those from Rotary Club, Kiwanis, Art Club, and so on).

☐ Drawn insight from past scholarship winners.

☐ Considered hiring a private financial aid counselor.

The Least You Need to Know

◆ The costs of a college education vary dramatically from institution to institution and from state to state. However, any education carries a hefty price tag, so planning early is essential to giving your child the greatest number of educational options.

◆ When estimating college costs, remember that tuition represents only about 40 percent of the full cost of college, which may also include room, board, and books. Also remember that you don't have to foot the bill alone.

◆ 529 funds are state or institution-sponsored plans that enable you to save money for future college costs. Invested savings accumulate earnings tax-free and disbursements for college costs are federally tax-free as well.

◆ Scholarships, grants, and student loans are some of the other options available for funding college costs. Work-study plans enable your child to accumulate college tuition funds while gaining experience working in public service efforts here or abroad.

Chapter 14

Planning for Retirement and Financial Independence

In This Chapter

◆ How much will your retirement lifestyle cost?

◆ Getting your retirement accounts in order

◆ Planning for guaranteed income

◆ Deciding when to start drawing from your retirement plan

◆ Long-term care for your finances

When you're 28 years old, stashing away $5,000 a year in a retirement plan can seem like a horrible waste of good, green cash. But, that pile of retirement dough will seem incredibly comforting when you fall out of the workforce and into retirement. There's nothing I can say here that you haven't already heard about the need for planning your retirement savings, so I won't bother with the lectures.

All of you smart people who are still with me in this chapter are about to learn how to use some very simple—yet effective—tools for keeping your retirement plans in order and working for you. The worksheets in this chapter will help you analyze your retirement needs, organize your retirement accounts, parse out your guaranteed income flow, and weigh the pros and cons of pre-mature distribution of retirement savings, so you can plan for the type of retirement you want to live.

Everyone will retire one day. The work you accomplish in this chapter will help make your last day of work the start of a new adventure—not the beginning of the end. Let the folks who skipped the whole retirement planning thing figure out how to live on Social Security—you won't have to.

What Does Retirement Mean to You?

The first step in planning your approach to retirement savings is to determine what kind of retirement you'd like to live. Many folks have a list of retirement to-do's all lined up:

- Travel

- Spend more time visiting the kids

- Volunteer

- Throw away professional wardrobe and replace with day-of-the-week sweatsuits

Whatever your particular retirement dreams might include, there's one thing I can tell you with almost dead certainty: your retirement life will be more expensive than your working life.

Okay, I can hear your objections even now (I've heard many from my new clients). "Are you kidding? I won't have the cost of my commute, I won't have to buy (and dry clean) all of those suits, I'll have more time to cook at home in place of eating out, I'll hand make all of the gifts I give … and don't forget all of the senior citizen price-breaks I'll be hauling in!" The truth is however, that most retirees find that none of these things results in a decrease in their cost of living. Instead, they discover that they fill much of their newly available time spending money.

If you doubt that you'd fall into that category, just take a look at your ATM withdrawals and when they occur. If you're like most people, you make the most withdrawals on days you're not working. Traveling, going to movies, buying things for those visits with the kids—you need to assume that you'll do some (or all) of these typical retiree time-fillers. As you age, the cost of medical care can escalate. And don't forget about inflation; that will definitely raise your expenses. Unfortunately, things people do for pleasure typically inflate at a higher rate than the average CPI (Consumer Price Index) inflation rate. So retirement is a nice thing, but, as the old saying goes, the nicer the nice, the higher the price.

My most important piece of advice for you when planning for your retirement needs is to be realistic and assume you'll spend more money than you do now. You can't necessarily predict how much more money you'll *choose* to spend, but you can predict the impact of inflation on your expenses.

 Pitfall Alert!

Don't fall for any of those rules of thumb for calculating how much you'll need in retirement. You know, the ones that say, "Count on needing 70 percent of your current income." Those generalities are worthless. Do your own careful assessment of what you'll need for the retirement you want to have.

Use the Retirement Expenses Analyzer to list your current monthly expenses and calculate inflationary changes. You've already listed most of these expenses in the Cash Flow Analysis worksheet back in Chapter 3. As you fill in the expense listings in the Retirement Expenses Analyzer, you can choose to add 10 percent or so to those expenses that you suspect you may bump up during retirement (for example, Vacation—Travel, Entertainment, Home Repair, or other services you may hire more often than do yourself). Fill in the number of years until your retirement, and your estimate of the inflation rate for each item. Inflation runs about 4 percent for most expenses, but as you can see in the sample worksheet, you might want to assume a higher rate for things such as Auto—Fuel and Medical Expenses. With all of that information in place, the analyzer will calculate the inflationary change in your total expenses after retirement.

Setting Up Your Retirement Accounts

After you retire, your income is likely to originate from pensions, savings, investments, and Social Security. For many Americans, "pension" has become synonymous with "401K." I've said it before, but it's worth saying again: one of the smartest things you can do to plan for your retirement is to participate in your employer's 401K plan—especially if your employer is matching your contributions (What? You want to walk away from free money?). Use all of the information I provided back in Chapters 8 and 9 to set up and manage those accounts as profitably as possible, and let your money work so that you, at some point in your life, won't have to.

A	B	C	D	E	F	G
1		**Retirement Expenses Analyzer**				
2						
3						
4 Years Until Retirement		24				
5						
6		Estimated				Estimated
7		Current		Inflation		Retirement
8 Expense		Expenses		Rate		Expenses
9						
10 Auto - Fuel		$ 200		5.0%		$ 645
11 Auto - Insurance		115		4.0%		295
12 Auto - Other		25		4.0%		64
13 Auto - Registration		10		4.0%		26
14 Cash / Miscellaneous		250		4.0%		641
15 Cell Phone		40		4.0%		103
16 Charity		50		4.0%		128
17 Childcare		500		4.0%		1,282
18 Children's Activities		75		4.0%		192
19 Children's Clothing		75		4.0%		192
20 Clothing		100		4.0%		256
21 Dining		75		4.0%		192
22 Entertainment		150		4.0%		384
23 Groceries		600		4.0%		1,538
24 Home Improvement		100		4.0%		256
25 Home Repair		100		4.0%		256
26 Insurance - Home		40		4.0%		103
27 Insurance - Life		75		4.0%		192
28 Landscaping - Yardwork		100		4.0%		256
29 Medical Expenses		61		6.0%		247
30 Mortgage / Rent		1,200		4.0%		3,076
31 Personal Care		50		4.0%		128
32 Subscriptions		10		4.0%		26
33 Taxes / Escrow		300		4.0%		769
34 Transportation Expenses		10		4.0%		26
35 Utilities - Cable TV		40		4.0%		103
36 Utilities - Garbage & Recycling		25		4.0%		64
37 Utilities - Gas & Electric		150		4.0%		384
38 Utilities - Internet		30		4.0%		77
39 Utilities - Telephone		60		4.0%		154
40 Utilities - Water		10		4.0%		26
41 Vacation - Travel		300		4.0%		769
42 Retirement - Vacation		-		4.0%		-
43 Retirement - Health Insurance		-		4.0%		-
44						
45 Total Expenses		$ 4,926				$ 12,850
46						

If you're self-employed, you aren't left out of the retirement plan bonanza. You have plenty of options beyond a simple IRA for setting up a retirement account. You can set up your own pension plan or profit-sharing plan. A Keogh plan, for example, is a tax-deferred savings plan for self-employed individuals. With the right investment advice (and adequate income) you can legally stash as much as $45,000 a year into tax-smart retirement savings. And that's for you young investors. As you reach age 50 and beyond, you can put up to a couple of hundred thousand dollars a year into your own pension plan, and reap the tax benefits.

In the Know _____

You self-employed folks might not want to go it alone in setting up your retirement accounts. See a financial advisor (Chapter 16 tells you more about choosing and using professional advisors). For a fast look at your possibilities, Uncle Sam publishes the annual limits online at www. irs.gov/newsroom/article/ 0,,id=187833,00.html.

As I mentioned earlier, remember that your 401K (or 403b, if you work for a public school or other tax-exempt organization) is merely a wallet that holds your investment vehicles. In addition to this collection of retirement investments, you might also have an employer-sponsored pension from previous employment, an IRA (Roth or regular), or a Keogh plan.

If you are single and your employer doesn't sponsor its own retirement plan, in 2008 you could contribute as much as $5,000 a year to a traditional IRA if you were under age 50, $6,000, if you were 50 or older (these limits are set to rise by $500 every year). Under most situations, you can contribute money to a traditional IRA and deduct every dollar of your contribution from your income taxes. You pay the taxes later, when you withdraw the money from the IRA at retirement (sometime around age 70), at the tax rate you're paying when you make the withdrawal.

Roth IRAs also have limitations and conditions for investors, but in general, these plans differ because your contributions to the plan are not tax-deferred, but qualified distributions from the plan are untaxed. You pay the taxes today, but you *don't* pay taxes later, when you withdraw the funds—no taxes, nada, not even on the money your investment has earned over the years!

You can use the Retirement Account Tracker to list all of your retirement plans and to record such important information as beneficiary names, periodic balance tallies, and your annual contribution amounts, as well as those of your employer. You need to periodically review your retirement accounts to make sure that they still match your goals, and this worksheet will save you a lot of time and headache in that process.

	A	B	C	D	E	F	G
1	**Retirement Account Tracker**						
2							
3							
4		Account Type	Owner	Beneficiary	Balance at MM/DD/YYYY	My Annual Contribution	Employer Contribution
5							
6		IRA					
7		403b					
8		401K					
9		Keogh					
10		Pension					
11		Roth 401K					
12		Roth IRA					

Planning for Guaranteed Income

Your retirement is almost certain to involve some type of guaranteed income, such as Social Security, a pension plan, and/or certain types of annuities (you learned about annuities back in Chapter 10).

The Social Security Administration (SSA) tells us that we should anticipate that Social Security will provide about 40 percent of our necessary income after retirement, and that figure could be somewhat optimistic depending on your cost of living. The SSA also has assured us that if we don't fix the funding shortfalls in Social Security, its funds could be exhausted by 2042. In any event, you shouldn't count on your benefits for any more than that 40 percent projection range, and a lower percentage might be even more realistic.

The amount of your Social Security retirement is determined by your lifetime income or your spouse's lifetime income (if you intend to collect a spousal benefit instead of your individual benefit), your year of birth, and the age at which you retire. If you're working and contributing to Social Security, you probably receive an annual notification of your projected monthly benefit amount. Be sure to check the earnings statements you receive from the SSA carefully, to be certain that your earnings are accurately recorded. The amount of your benefit is dependent in part on your earnings, so the accuracy of your earnings record is important. But you can check on your projected benefits any time by visiting the SSA's website (www.ssa.gov) and using the agency's Retirement Estimator.

Depending on your birth date, the full retirement age at which you can start drawing those Social Security checks is age 65 (if you were born in 1937 or earlier),

In the Know

Social Security isn't just for retirees. Others who collect Social Security benefits might include Americans with disabilities, spouses or children of individuals who currently collect Social Security, and spouses, children, or parents of deceased workers.

66 (if born between 1943 and 1954), or 67 (for those born in 1967 or later), with incremental upticks in the intervening years (visit www.pueblo.gsa.gov for a detailed chart). The longer you delay in collecting these payments, the higher your monthly benefit becomes. You can start collecting payments early, at age 62, but your monthly benefit is permanently reduced if you do. You can continue to work while receiving benefits, but your benefit amount will be reduced until you reach full retirement age. After that, your earnings do not reduce your benefit amount.

Pitfall Alert! _____

Even if you decide to wait until age 70 to begin drawing Social Security benefits, you should apply for Medicare (the Federal government's subsidized health care insurance program) immediately when you reach age 65. Your premium costs may increase if you apply for Medicare more than three months after your sixty-fifth birthday.

So what about those other guaranteed income sources? You can start withdrawing money from your 401K, IRAs, and most tax-deferred pension plans at age 59½ without penalties (I talk about premature distributions in the next section of this chapter). Most retirement accounts have different restrictions and benefits, based on your employer-sponsored retirement plan.

If you are invested in annuities, you will have determined the time frame during which you will begin receiving distributions in just about any format you want, from lump sums to guaranteed income for life. Many folks mistakenly believe that annuities only provide a regular stream of income, but that's just one possibility. Although you can use annuities to turn a lump sum of cash into a stream of income, you also can cash out the annuity for a single payment. Annuities are guaranteed by the insurance company who issued them, so make sure you buy from a fiscally, financially strong insurance company with good ratings.

No matter what guaranteed income sources you have, you need to educate yourself about their conditions, limitations, and projected benefit amounts. You can use the Guaranteed Income Scheduler to list your guaranteed income sources, benefit amounts, and projected start dates. Like other schedules and trackers in this workbook, you need to keep this document up to date. Most importantly, don't just assume that your retirement is all taken care of. There aren't many guarantees in life, even when it comes to guaranteed retirement income.

	A	B	C	D
1	**Guaranteed Income Scheduler**	**Source**	**Amount**	**Start Date**
2				
3				
4				
5		Social Security Income		
6		Defined Benefit Pension		
7		Annuity Income		
8		Other Guaranteed Income		

Retirement Plan Distributions

You aren't required to take out your retirement savings (IRA and pension) until the year after you hit the age of 70½. As I mentioned earlier, age 59½ is the earliest at which you can start drawing benefits without paying penalties, unless you're totally disabled. If you die before reaching age 59½, your beneficiaries can withdraw your tax-deferred savings without any age-related penalties. A smart beneficiary would consult with a financial advisor to discuss the benefits of taking as little as possible from this account and letting as much as possible grow tax-deferred.

You can opt to access your retirement savings early, and the monthly benefit amount will be reduced to stretch out your total disbursement over your expected lifetime. So, even if you are 51 years old, you could start receiving retirement distributions, but they would be reduced to account for a longer period of disbursal (these are called *Section 72t distributions*). Once you start getting premature distributions, you can stop until you reach age 59½. Then, the monthly benefit amount will be reduced, as well, to accommodate the early payments you've already received.

def•i•ni•tion

Section 72t of the IRS code states that funds withdrawn from a traditional or Roth IRA are designated as premature withdrawals, and subject to income tax and early withdrawal fines of as much as 10 percent of the amount of the distribution. That's why these withdrawals are called **Section 72t distributions.**

The Premature Distribution Cost and Penalty Calculator can help you calculate the cost of early withdrawal from your tax-deferred retirement accounts. Fill in the total amount of the early withdrawal, and your Federal and State income tax bracket/rate. The Calculator will determine your tax and early withdrawal penalty payments.

	A	B	C
1	**Premature Distribution Cost and Penalty Calculator**		
2			
3			
4	Withdrawal Amount		$ 20,000
5	Federal Income Tax Bracket		20%
6	State Income Tax Rate		5%
7			
8	Federal Income Taxes Paid		$ 4,000
9	State Income Taxes Paid		1,000
10	10% Early Withdrawal Penalty		200
11			
12	Total Cost of Premature Distribution		$ 5,200

Making Your Money Last as Long as You Do

Great news, everyone! Thanks to the wonders of modern medicine, improved sanitation, etcetera, etcetera, etcetera, we're all going to live a lot longer than did previous generations. Bad news, everyone! We're also going to outpace every previous generation in the mileage we'll have to get out of our retirement funds. Who wants to be the world's oldest homeless person?

You can't open a newspaper or magazine without finding advice on how to stretch your retirement dollars, and you're probably so far from retirement right now that you aren't interested in more of that advice (and you'll forget a lot of what you learn today during your 50s, anyway). But I do want to offer three pieces of important information on this topic that you should try not to forget:

1. Be careful not to use too much of your retirement savings too soon. No one knows what "too soon" will be for them, because no one knows how long they'll live or what kinds of economic surprises life holds in store. But you can keep a careful watch on your investments' annual earnings and how they're contributing to your nest egg. You can also use the Nest Egg Estimators you first learned about in Chapter 9 to calculate how your funds will play out during your retirement years.

2. Remember that you can lock in guaranteed income through annuities or other fixed income investments, but—because these might, in some cases, pay lower interest rates than other types of investments—you may be locking in a lower rate of return forever. Also, when you convert a pile of money into an income stream, you no longer have access to that pile. Maybe the security of a guaranteed stream of income compensates for that lack of access and the potential for reduced returns, but be aware of these factors when considering these investments.

3. Your investments may grow at your projected rates of return, and they may lose at unpredictable rates of loss. How you invest your retirement assets should always be consistent with your needs, time frame, and tolerance for risk.

The Least You Need to Know

♦ Many people actually spend *more* after retirement, because they have more free time in which to spend money and as a result of inflation.

♦ Your retirement accounts might include an employer-sponsored pension, 401K or 403b plan, IRAs, or other retirement savings and investment programs. Review your retirement accounts periodically to make sure they still match your investment and retirement goals.

♦ Guaranteed retirement income can include Social Security benefits, pensions, annuities, or other plans. Review carefully (and regularly) the projected benefit payments of any guaranteed plan you will be relying on for income during your retirement.

♦ In most cases, you can start withdrawing retirement benefits early, but your regular benefit payouts will be reduced to account for your longer period of withdrawal.

♦ Your retirement funds have to last as long as you do, so don't take out too much, too soon. Take into account the potential for reduced returns and other restrictions of some guaranteed income investments, and consider how much increased income you're willing to sacrifice for the security of a guaranteed income stream.

15

You Can't Take It with You: Estate Planning

In This Chapter

◆ What you need to know about estate planning

◆ Your will, your way

◆ Do you need a trust?

◆ Taking care of others

◆ Death and taxes

◆ It's never too late

If you're preparing to flip through these pages to the next chapter of this book, I recommend that you stop now and read this chapter. Everyone who reads this book needs to understand the basics of estate planning. Really.

If you're single, just establishing yourself in your first job, living in a studio apartment furnished with a futon and three milk crates, have no living relatives, no savings, no investments, and no debt, okay, you can just skim through this chapter. But, you still need to know the basics of what happens to your possessions and obligations after your death. Besides, most people don't fit into that profile I just described. And for those of us who own anything or who have any chance of ever inheriting anything from any one else—or who have parents who may need help with *their* estate planning—it's important that we understand the fundamentals of the estate planning process.

The lists, questionnaires, and worksheets in this chapter will help you lock down those basics. You can use them to document your own estate issues and wishes; to plan for your inheritance; to evaluate the thoroughness of your will; to understand the issues surrounding trusts; to create a plan that will help others take care of you, your children, and/or aged parents, should you become incapacitated; and to manage (and minimize) estate taxes. Your estate plan must address all of these issues and more—a will isn't enough.

I've packed a lot of information into this chapter, and you might not feel a burning need to absorb all of it right now. But you'll need this information one day—that's an inescapable truth.

Who Owns What? Making a Plan

An estate plan outlines the *disposition* of your estate—what will happen to your property, investments, and legal obligations after your death. If your estate plan doesn't include a will, when you pass away or become disabled in a way that makes you incompetent or prevents you from communicating with others, the state steps in (an event the legal types refer to as *intestacy*). Under state rules called *laws of intestacy*, your assets will be distributed and governed by your state of legal residence. Every state has its own rules, but if you die intestate, those rules will … well, rule. It doesn't matter if you're married or have close living relatives or told everyone at happy hour last Friday that you wanted your cubicle-mate Stan to have your collection of early '70s glam-rock vinyl if anything ever happened to you, state rules of intestacy will prevail. And, since you're reading this book, I am almost certain that you don't want the state to decide what to do with your estate.

def•i•ni•tion

If you die without an estate plan or will, you are legally described as having died **intestate**. Every state has its own **intestacy laws** that govern the **disposition**, or the distribution of, the property of those who die without a will.

You can find a quick guide to every state's laws of intestacy on your estate at www. mystatewill.com. The site even offers a calculator to help calculate the impact of any state's laws on your estate. And remember, you can avoid all of that intestacy business along with a host of other problems by making an estate plan. If you have children, an estate plan is an absolute must. You might think that your sister and her husband will gladly take on the raising of your kids if you and your spouse meet a tragic end, but what happens if they can't—or won't? Estate planning gives you an opportunity to consider *every* contingency and to discuss your expectations, wishes, and legal stipulations in advance. That way, you aren't leaving a legal swamp for your loved ones to slog through while they're trying to cope with your loss.

Understanding Ownership

Before you begin doling out your property, it's worth your while to take a quick look at the whole subject of ownership. We're talking about legalities here, not that dreamy "what's mine is yours" promise you might have made over drinks with your fiancé (or college roommate). You can't give away something that isn't really yours, and you can't legally transfer ownership of most property through a casual conversation. Not only that, laws governing ownership may override the wishes you set forth in your estate plan and will, so it's important that you understand them before you draw up either document.

The Ownership Structure Organizer lists and describes legal forms of ownership. As you read through this listing, check all forms of ownership that apply to you and your estate, so you understand what types of structures you'll need to account for in your estate plan.

Drawing Up a Plan

An estate plan needs to cover a wealth of issues (even if you're not wealthy). I've collected all of these issues into a single estate planning document. But before we get to that, let me just tick through some of the considerations you'll be making when you complete the Estate Planning Questionnaire that's coming up in a moment.

	A	B	C	D
1	Ownership Structure Organizer	Form of Ownership	Characteristics	Applicable to Your Estate
2				
3				
4		Individual	In your name only. Property is subject to the claims of any creditors or litigation you may encounter.	
5		Joint Ownership with Rights of Survivorship	You are a co-owner whereby your interest automatically transfers to your joint owner upon your death. The property is subject to the claims of either owner's creditors or lawsuits.	
6		Joint Tenants in Common	You own a divided interest in the property. Your ownership interest will pass to your designated recipient under your will upon your death. The property is subject to the claims of either owner's creditors or lawsuits.	
7		Partnership	A partnership is for two or more owners. Each partner is jointly and severally liable for the actions, liabilities, and claims with respect to property owned by the partnership	
8		Corporation	A corporation can be owned by one or more owners. Property held inside a corporation may be protected from liabilities or litigation arising to you individually and outside of the corporation. You would be a shareholder of the corporation.	
9		Limited Liability Company or Partnership (LLC or LLP)	An LLC or LLP can be owned by one or more members. Property held inside these entities may be protected from liabilities or litigation arising to you individually and outside of the entity. Your ownership interest in the entity is called a members interest.	
10		Trust	A trust has two important ownership characteristics. The trustee is the person or entity who is the fiduciary required to act in accordance with the terms of the trust for the benefit of the beneficiaries. The beneficiary(s) is the person or entity for whom the property is maintained. Depending on trust design and objectives, ownership in a trust may or may not protect assets from creditors or litigation arising to you individually and outside of the trust.	

Understand that your estate plan doesn't replace your will as a legal document. Your will is simply a part of your overall estate plan. In the next section of this chapter, we dig into the details of writing a will, in which you'll legally assign beneficiaries, executors, administrators, and so on. For now, just remember that you need to list all of this information in your estate plan, as well. You need to update your estate plan regularly to keep it current with your financial, family, and legal life. Also, do your heirs or associates a big favor and keep a copy of all legal documents and the previous year's tax returns with your estate plan.

Here is a rundown of the categories of information you'll be working with in the Estate Planning Questionnaire, and some quick notes on completing those sections of your plan:

- **Basic information:** This section lists the facts of who you are, where you live and work, and some critical information about details such as any deposit boxes you own, any inheritances on your own horizon, and any *powers of appointment* floating around out there with your name on them.

def•i•ni•tion

Powers of appointment give an individual the right to decide how to distribute another person's property. These powers are typically assigned in wills, trusts, and other legal documents of ownership.

- **Marital history:** In this section, you'll list current and prior marriages, and detail any continuing obligations for the latter. You'll also list information about your current and past state residency, since some states have specific laws regarding property rights for ex-spouses.

- **Family:** Here, you'll list details about your children and their current residence and marital status, and whether (and how) you want to divide your estate among them. You'll also be asked about mentally or physically disabled family members, as well as any other family members that you want to list as beneficiaries.

- **Desired disposition of estate:** This is a simple table in which you say how you want your estate divided among your beneficiaries, and any terms or timing that you want to apply to the divvying up.

- **Documents:** Here, you list wills, trusts, pre- or post-nuptial agreements, divorces, and other legal agreements bearing your name.

♦ **Retirement, disability, and death benefit:** In this section, list all of your pensions, profit-sharing plans, stock bonuses, self-employment retirement plans, and so on. You'll also list and outline your annuities and life insurance policies. You have compiled all of this information in chapters 7 (insurance), 11 (investments), and 14 (retirement accounts), so listing it here will be easy. It also will make it a lot easier for those you leave behind to have all of this information in a single document.

def•i•ni•tion

Fiduciaries are the people you appoint to specific roles in your estate plan or will. An **executor** is the person you appoint to carry out the provisions of your will. A **trustee** manages any trusts you establish. A **guardian** is someone you've appointed to care for you, your dependents, or property, including whomever you've given durable power of attorney (described in Chapter 4).

♦ **Fiduciaries:** The term *fiduciaries* simply refers to the *executors*, *trustees*, and *guardians* you wish to appoint to handle your estate. This section holds columns for both spouses, where you can list these individuals, their contact information, and whether you want them to serve as co-fiduciaries or as successors should your first appointment be unable to fulfill his or her role. Make sure you talk to every fiduciary you list in your estate plan to make sure they understand and are willing to accept the responsibilities of their appointment. And, again, revisit your fiduciary choices regularly to be sure they're still viable.

♦ **Advisors:** Last, you will need to list all of the financial planners and advisors you work with—the worksheet even has space for you to list insurance agents, clergy, and physicians.

♦ **Summaries of assets and liabilities:** You can use the detailed listings of your assets and liabilities that you completed in Chapter 1 to fill in these sections of the Estate Planning Questionnaire. Again, it's a good idea to keep all of this information together, so people don't have to scramble for it after you're gone.

Estate Planning Questionnaire

Client: _____

Attorney: _____   Referred by: _____

I. BASIC INFORMATION

	CLIENT	**SPOUSE**

Legal name and other names
known by: _____   _____

                             _____   _____

Social Security No.   _____   _____

Status of Health   _____   _____

Citizenship   _____   _____

Occupation   _____   _____

Employer   _____   _____

Employer Address   _____   _____

                             _____   _____

Work Telephone   _____   _____

Home Telephone   _____   _____

Home Address: _____

E-Mail Address: _____

Correspondence to: _____

Safe Deposit Box? Yes ___ No___ Location: _____

Any possibility of an inheritance? Yes ___ No___

If yes, list source and amount: _____

continues

continued

Parental support obligation? Yes ___ No___

If yes, list name(s), age(s), and amount:

_____

Any "powers of appointment" under any existing wills or trusts usually from other family members?

Yes ___ No___ Not Sure___

II. MARITAL HISTORY

Date of marriage: _____

Any prior marriages? If so, please provide dates: _____

Continuing obligations? Describe: _____

_____

Years of residence in present state: _____

During marriage, have you ever lived in (please circle appropriate states): Arizona, California, Idaho, Louisiana, Nevada, New Mexico, Texas, Washington, or Wisconsin? Yes ___ No ___

III. FAMILY

List Children/Grandchildren:

Name	City/ST	DOB	SS#	Married (y/n)	Child/GC
1.					
2.					
3.					
4.					
5.					

More space provided on last page

NOTE: *Indicate whether any of above are children from prior marriages.*

Any possibility of additional natural or adopted children? Yes ___ No ___

Any deceased children? If so, please provide details:

_____

_____

_____

_____

Is anyone in your family mentally or physically disabled? _____

If so, please describe:

_____

_____

_____

_____

Do you support any of these family members? Yes ___ No ___

Do you want property eventually divided equally between all children? Yes ___ No ___

If no, please explain:

_____

_____

_____

_____

List any other individuals you wish to be beneficiaries of your estate:

Name	**City/ST**	**Relationship**	**Age**	**Married (y/n)**
1.				
2.				
3.				
4.				

continues

continued

5. _____

IV. <u>DESIRED DISPOSITION OF ESTATE</u>

	Timing	Terms	Amount or %
Children			
Grandchildren			
Other			
Charity			

V. <u>DOCUMENTS</u>

1. Wills   Yes ___ No ___ Date: _____

2. Trusts   Yes ___ No ___ Date: _____

3. Pre- or Post-nuptial Agreement   Yes ___ No ___ Date: _____

4. Divorce Agreement   Yes ___ No ___ Date: _____

5. Separation Agreement   Yes ___ No ___ Date: _____

6. Prior Gift Tax Returns   Yes ___ No ___ Date: _____

7. Shareholder Agreement   Yes ___ No ___ Date: _____

8. Partnership Agreement   Yes ___ No ___ Date: _____

9. Irrevocable Trusts   Yes ___ No ___ Date: _____

10. Other: _____

* * * PLEASE FURNISH COPIES OF ABOVE DOCUMENTS * * *
AND LAST YEAR'S INCOME TAX RETURN

VI. <u>RETIREMENT, DISABILITY, AND DEATH BENEFITS</u>
(e.g., pension, profit sharing, stock bonus, self-employed retirement plan, IRA, deferred comp. plan)

Name of Company and Plan	Current Value	Beneficiary and Payment Options Available

Annuities

Name of Company	Current Value	Beneficiary & Payment Options Available

Life Insurance

Company & Policy #	Type* Annual Premium	Name of Insured	Name of Owner	Names of Primary & Contingent Beneficiaries	Face Value	Cash Value	Loan Balance

* Group term, individual term, ordinary (whole life), split dollar, accidental death, travel, etc.

continues

continued

VI. FIDUCIARIES (proposed Executors, Trustees, and Guardians)

For Executors and Trustees, you can appoint (1) your spouse, (2) another relative, (3) any other individual in whom you have confidence, (4) a trust company [usually with a local office], or (5) a combination of any of the above as co-fiduciaries.

After naming the initial fiduciary, indicate whether any following fiduciary is to be a Co-fiduciary ("C") or a Successor fiduciary ("S").

Include address and relationship for fiduciaries.

	Husband	**Wife**

EXECUTORS:

TRUSTEES:

GUARDIANS (Guardians required in event that both of you should die while any child is a minor):

DURABLE POWER OF ATTORNEY:

_____   _____

_____   _____

Health Care Agent: _____

VII. <u>ADVISORS</u>

	<u>NAME</u>	<u>ADDRESS</u>	<u>TELEPHONE</u>

Accountant: _____

Trust Officer: _____

Commercial Banker: _____

Investment Advisor: _____

Financial Planner: _____

Stockbroker: _____

Life Insurance Agent: _____

Casualty Insurance Agent: _____

Clergyman: _____

Physician: _____

continues

continued

SUMMARY OF ASSETS & LIABILITIES

ASSETS	Husband	Wife	Joint
Automobiles	_____	_____	_____
Automobile Loan	_____	_____	_____
Tangible Personal Property (jewelry, furniture, etc.)	_____	_____	_____
Residence	_____	_____	_____
Residential 1st Mortgage	_____	_____	_____
Residential Equity Mortgage	_____	_____	_____
Other Real Estate	_____	_____	_____
Other Real Estate Mortgage	_____	_____	_____
Cash, Bank Accounts, and CDs	_____	_____	_____
Notes, Accounts, and Mortgages Receivable	_____	_____	_____
Bonds	_____	_____	_____
Listed Stocks/Mutual Funds	_____	_____	_____
Closely Held Stock	_____	_____	_____
Partnerships	_____	_____	_____
IRA's/401Ks/SEP IRAs	_____	_____	_____
Annuities	_____	_____	_____
Retirement Plan Benefits	_____	_____	_____
Life Insurance Cash Value	_____	_____	_____
Other: _____	_____	_____	_____
TOTAL ASSETS	_____	_____	_____

LIABILITIES	Husband	Wife	Joint
Credit Cards	_____	_____	_____
Promissory Notes Owing	_____	_____	_____
Other Debts	_____	_____	_____
TOTAL LIABILITIES	_____	_____	_____
NET WORTH (ASSETS – LIABILITIES)	_____	_____	_____
Insurance (Face Value)	_____	_____	_____
TOTAL NET ASSETS	_____	_____	_____

Additional space for children, grandchildren and other notes:

_____

_____

_____

_____

_____

_____

_____

_____

What Happens When You Inherit?

You might be in line for an inheritance of your own. If so, planning for that is part of creating an effective estate plan. Your inheritance might become your beneficiaries' inheritance, so you need to spell out what it is and what's to happen to it.

Maybe you'll decide, for example, that you really don't *want* your Aunt Etta's mobile home down in the Chain O' Lakes retirement community in Florida, so perhaps she should leave it to your sister who just loves being around retirees. Or maybe you think it should be sold and the proceeds divvied up between your nieces and nephews. In any event, you need to think through all of the ramifications of any inheritance you might receive and spell out what you want to be done with it, should you be unable to make that decision some day.

The Planning for Inheritance Checklist will walk you through a series of questions that will help you consider all of those ramifications and decisions. Check the box next to each question for which your answer is "yes," then go back to your Estate Planning Questionnaire and make sure that it includes your wishes for the disposition of your inheritance (you can list details in the Other line of the Assets section of the Questionnaire and in the notes section at the end of that document).

Working with Wills

Are you immortal? If so, put in a good word for me with all of your neighbors up there on Mt. Olympus. If not, you need a will. A will is a legal document that declares a person's wishes in regard to what happens to that individual's property after he or she dies. Not having a current will is negligent, no matter how little property you own.

Pitfall Alert!

I know there are plenty of free, pre-fab wills out there, but I advise you to have an estate attorney draw up or at least finalize your will. This document will be subject to legal interpretation after you're gone, and if you've left anything out or garbled something or miscommunicated your wishes, your will isn't worth the ink it's printed with.

Before you toddle off to the estate attorney's office (and, I recommend that you find an estate attorney for this process) to lock down your will, you need to prepare to provide some information. The attorney will ask you to designate beneficiaries and administrators. In the Estate Planning Questionnaire you listed those folks, but now, I want to talk about those choices in a bit more detail.

Planning for Inheritance Checklist

☐   Am I aware of any expected inheritances?

☐   Do I need or want the inherited property?

☐   Would it be better if the property to be inherited was bequeathed to someone else?

- ○ A sibling?
- ○ An offspring?
- ○ A charity?

☐   Should I consider disclaiming the inheritance?

☐   Do all beneficiaries know of the expected inheritance?

☐   Are any assets to be split with other beneficiaries inherently difficult to divide?

- ○ Real estate
- ○ Family business
- ○ Artwork
- ○ Collectibles
- ○ Personal effects such as jewelry

☐   Do the beneficiaries have a plan on how to divide those assets difficult to divide?

☐   Will all beneficiaries be able to support and maintain jointly inherited assets such as vacation property?

☐   Are there any qualified plans or IRAs to be inherited?

☐   Will any property inherited need special assistance or qualified professionals to handle, value, or maintain?

☐   Will I need to sell any inherited assets?

Choosing Beneficiaries

The beneficiaries you assign in your will are the folks who you want to take possession of your possessions after your death. This might seem like a no-brainer: "When I die, split everything I own between my brother and sister." Or, "My spouse gets everything after I die." But I advise you to take a minute to think these decisions over with a bit more care.

Splitting it all evenly between your siblings might not be a completely logical choice, for example, if your sister is an orthopedic surgeon who pulls in half-a-mil a year, and your brother is working with the Peace Corps in Zimbabwe. Or, you leave everything to your wife, but what about that coin collection that you've promised to your cousin? What if your spouse remarries, or what happens if she dies after you? Are you satisfied to leave your family heirlooms to whatever member of her extended family is left to dispose of her estate?

Pitfall Alert!

Keep your beneficiary designations current. If you leave everything to your first husband, your second husband might be somewhat angry if you fail to update your beneficiaries with his name. Life changes on a regular basis, so your will has to be kept up-to-date through all of your personal evolutions.

You get the point, I'm sure. Before you assign beneficiaries, you need to consider all of the ramifications for those decisions and make sure your will includes terms and language that accommodates them. Your attorney will help you with this process, so be sure to fill out the Schedule of Beneficiary Designations worksheet and take it with you for your appointment. That way, you'll have a listing to work through as your attorney asks you about specific provisions for each beneficiary.

	A	B	C	D	E	F
1			Schedule of Beneficiary Designations			
2						
3			Life Insurance Policies	Retirement Plans	Trusts	Other
4						
5		Primary Beneficiary(s)				
6		Secondary Beneficiary(s)				

Designating Executors and Guardians

In the Estate Planning Questionnaire you listed the executors and guardians for your estate plan who officially get appointed in your will. If your parents have a will, they might have designated you to be the executor (and if they don't have a will, you can help them fix that tragedy-waiting-to-happen with the information you're learning here).

Wills typically name three types of fiduciaries: executors, trustees, and guardians, which I talked about earlier in the chapter. Executors are those responsible for carrying out the wishes you've expressed in your will. A guardian is an individual you've assigned to care for you, your dependents, or your property. You might be named as an executor or guardian in your parents' wills (if so, I hope they've discussed those responsibilities with you).

Choose executors and guardians carefully. Many parents assume that their eldest child should be the executor of their will, but birthright and age aren't necessarily qualifiers for the role of executor. Executors have executive duties to fulfill, including settling your estate, taking inventories, moving your estate through probate, filing estate taxes, inheritance taxes, and the decedent's final 1040 tax form. Birthright and age don't matter nearly as much as the individual's ability to pay attention to details and devote time to executive duties.

Taxes are a central responsibility of will executors. If you die prior to paying your taxes for the current year, your estate still owes a tax return and possible tax payments for that year. Your executor is personally liable for making sure your taxes are filed properly. That's why lawyers often wait for nine months or so to recommend the distribution of estate assets; they want to make sure the executor didn't mess up the estate administration or tax filings and give them a bounce-back liability. States levy their own estate and inheritance taxes, in addition to the equivalent federal taxes, so executors have a lot to keep track of.

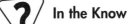 **In the Know**

Choose the individual who you feel is best suited—by judgment, geographic location, experience, lifestyle demands, and other conditions—to take on the role of executor. And don't make the decision legal until you've discussed the role with the individual you're considering. Maybe your sister doesn't *want* to be in charge of selling your Barbie doll collection.

Be careful when choosing guardians for your children, pets, or property, as well. Guardians may be taking on a lifelong caretaker's role, and you want to be sure that you feel confident that the qualities and conditions that make you lean toward choosing a particular guardian today are likely to endure. If your brother lost his job, would he be likely to bounce back and continue to provide a stable environment for your daughter? Your best friend says she will take your pets if anything were to happen to you, but will her husband agree?

When assigning guardianships that will extend for an indefinite period of time and require extensive attention and/or funds, you probably need to create a trust and assign a trustee, as well (I'll talk more about trusts later in this chapter). Your trustee will be responsible for carrying out the conditions of your trust.

In every case, communicate with administrators to tell them what their duties are, and why you've chosen them. If you have a *living will*, be certain to list all of these details in that document, as well. Also, remember to name a backup for every administrative role. That way, your overall plan won't suffer if one of your primary selections is unable to fulfill his or her duties.

def•i•ni•tion

A **living will** is a document that sets forth your wishes for administering your finances, estate, and health care wishes should you become incapacitated for some period of time before your death.

The Minor Children Needs Checklist will help you make sure you've attended to the necessary details. Use it and review it regularly. Any item that can't be checked off as a done-deal needs your immediate attention.

Minor Children Needs Checklist

☐ Have you made adequate provisions for any special health or educational needs your children might have?

☐ Would you like all of your children in the same household in the event of your premature death?

☐ Have you selected a guardian and back-up guardian in your will?

☐ Are you completely satisfied with your choice of guardian?

☐ Have you discussed this selection with your guardian?

☐ Do your children get along with the children of your selected guardian?

☐ Will the selected guardian have room in his or her home for your children?

☐ Will the selected guardian be paid for his or her services?

☐ Can the selected guardian afford to care for your children?

☐ Is your selected guardian willing to pay for the care of your children?

☐ Will the selected guardian have access to your insurance proceeds or other assets after your passing?

Is It Good Enough?

Is your will good enough? Here are some points to consider when making that decision:

◆ If, in spite of my earlier warning, you used a Last Will and Testament form you downloaded from luckylawyers.com, you can assume it isn't good enough.

◆ If you've had your will for more than 5 years, and never updated it, it might not be good enough.

◆ If you move to a new state, your old will *might* not be good enough. Check with an attorney in your new home state to determine whether your will is in synch with that state's laws.

In regard to that last item, be aware that the new attorney will probably want to redraft your will. Most attorneys are reluctant to put their stamp of approval on a legal document drawn up by another attorney. So, in fact, you may have to have a new will drafted every time you relocate to a new state. Yes, that's a drag, but it's better than having your will tossed out of court over some minor geographically determined legality.

To make sure your will remains up-to-date and on-target with your wishes, review it every few years, more often when you (or an administrator) has experienced changes that might impact the effectiveness of the document. Use the Will Evaluation Checklist to tick through the issues most likely to make that impact and require a will revision.

In the Know _____

Charges vary, of course, but in general, attorneys charge between $350 and $1,000 to draft a simple will. For a more complicated situation—a will that assigns durable power of attorney, health care powers, trusts, and so on—the charge might be more like $5,000.

Will Evaluation Checklist

☐ What is the date of your will?

☐ Have there been any major changes since its signing?

- Estate tax laws
- Family situation
- Special circumstances
- Asset appreciation or depreciation
- Asset acquisition or disposition

☐ Have you reviewed the document recently?

☐ Are you still satisfied with the provisions of your will?

☐ Are the executor or executrix choices still appropriate?

☐ Are the guardian choices still appropriate?

☐ Have you included spendthrift provisions to prevent children over 18 from inheriting too much money too soon?

☐ Have you provided adequate instructions for the disposition of personal property such as jewelry, artwork, or other personal items of value or emotional significance?

☐ Do you have any estranged children or other beneficiaries named under your will?

☐ Have you adequately prepared for the succession of any business interests?

Creating Trusts

A trust is a legal entity that owns funds or other property where the trustee oversees or manages the property for the benefit of another individual (the beneficiary). If you leave something behind that will need to be taken care of at some expense (a child, an art collection, a historic home), you can help ensure that care by leaving behind a trust with a dedicated trustee for that purpose.

Let's say, for example, that when you die you have two children, ages 9 and 13, and you have named your brother as their guardian. Your will also stipulates that your estate is to be divided evenly between the two boys. First, let's hope that you also stipulated in your will when this money was to be given to them. Without specific language, in most states the children will get your assets at age 18. Do you want them to have it right away (I hear all of the video game and car manufacturers out there shouting "yes!")? If not, maybe you stipulated that the money should be dispersed on their twenty-first birthdays, or even a more experienced age such as 30, 35, or 40 when they're old enough to handle it wisely.

But what happens in the meantime? To make sure your brother can access those funds if he needs money to help care for your children, you should set up a trust. Taking on two children isn't a cheap proposition. Your trust sets up funds for that purpose, and outlines conditions for the use of the funds. And, if you don't want your kids sharing a Harry Potter-like under-the-stairs bedroom, it's a good idea.

You need to have an attorney create your trust. If you're uncertain as to whether you need one, ask yourself these questions:

- ◆ Is my gross estate (including life insurance proceeds) greater than $2 million?

- ◆ Do I want to delay dispersing any inheritance to beneficiaries until they have reached a specific age?

- ◆ Do I want to place restrictions on or allow spending inheritance funds prior to dispersing them to beneficiaries?

- ◆ Do I want to put conditions on my beneficiary's ability to gain access to the inheritance (for example, at college graduation, when they get a full-time job, or only if they can manage to stay out of jail for three years straight)?

- ◆ Do my beneficiaries need assistance in managing the assets of my estate?

If you answered "yes" to *any* of these questions, a trust may be appropriate. Have your attorney draft the trust, then remember to review it regularly, just as you do all of your estate planning documents. You can use the Trust Evaluation Checklist to make sure you're covering your bases during this review.

Trust Evaluation Checklist

☐ What is the date of my trust?

☐ Have there been any major changes since its signing?

- ○ Personal
- ○ Estate tax laws
- ○ Health
- ○ With beneficiaries
- ○ Asset appreciation or depreciation
- ○ Asset acquisition or disposition

☐ Does my trust afford asset protection?

☐ Is the selection of trustee still appropriate?

☐ Have I selected an appropriate alternate trustee?

☐ Are the beneficiary elections still appropriate?

☐ Are the secondary beneficiary elections still appropriate?

☐ Are my assets currently owned by the trust?

Incapacity Planning

You might think I'm a ghoul, but I just can't help bringing up the subject of an incapacitating disability once again (we talked about various aspects of planning for disability back in Chapters 4, 7, and 13). When you make a will, you are planning the distribution of your estate in the most cost effective and efficient manner. But you still need to plan for problems which may arise during your lifetime that prevent you from managing your affairs for a period of time.

The primary objective of incapacity planning is the avoidance of the court-controlled guardianship system and its incumbent costs in time and money. You want to keep control of your finances, property, and health care decisions, if at all possible, within your family. If you aren't able to express your desires and direct your financial institutions as to what to do with your assets, then you lose control of your life. You need to appoint someone to step in and act on your behalf. Otherwise, you leave a control vacuum that the court system alone can fill. If you plan today, your children or dependent parents won't be faced with having to accept a court-appointed guardian.

The law gives you several options, which acting together can allow you to direct the control over your assets when you no longer are able to. We've already talked about many of those options—your will, a trust, durable power of attorney (we talked about that back in Chapter 4), and so on. The law also allows you to nominate a health care surrogate, someone who can make your health care decisions for you if you cannot. Each document addresses different aspects of the problem of incapacity. The Incapacity Planning Checklist lists a number of documents and plans you should have in place to protect yourself and your family. Check off each item that you have prepared for, and give attention to any item you can't check today.

Incapacity Planning Checklist

☐   Do I have current wills?

☐   Do I have current trusts?

☐   Do I have a durable power of attorney?

☐   Do I have a living will, health care surrogate, or health care power of attorney?

☐   Is a copy of my living will in the hands of my primary care physician?

☐   Do my heirs know the location of important documents?

☐   Do my heirs have a list of my doctors and other medical advisors?

☐   Do my heirs have a list of my financial, tax, and legal advisors?

☐   Do I have long-term care insurance?

☐   Do I have a plan for the care and maintenance of my home, pets, and personal items such as bill paying and mail service?

Review all of your plans—your wills, trusts, checklists, and Estate Planning Questionnaire—regularly, to be certain that they're all set up to establish control in the case of your incapacitation.

Before we leave this topic, let's talk for a minute about your parents. Many of us will be called upon to help our parents plan their estate, draw up their wills, and/or create trusts. But *all* of us need to make sure our parents have a thorough, reliable, and effective incapacity plan, as well. A number of factors determine what kind of incapacity plan is right for your parents. If you live near them, for example, their plan might rely more on your immediate care or medical permissions in case of an emergency, but might list nearby neighbors, family, or friends if you live far away or are unable to provide that care. If your parents are currently capable of taking care of themselves, their plan will deal with future incapacities, rather than immediate realities. Your parents' plan, like your own, needs ongoing review and revision to remain current and adequate to their needs.

Another important part of your incapacity planning—and that of your parents—is getting long-term care insurance. Most people don't think about insurance until they already need it, when it has become unavailable or too expensive to purchase. The best time to get long-term care insurance is when you're around age 50. It might cost you $1,000 a year or more. If you wait until you're 75, this insurance will cost $5,000 or more a year, and by age 85, it's not worth it. You might say, oh, I'll take care of my mother, so she doesn't need to pay for this care, or you might have a loving family member who makes the same promise to you. But if you or your parent suffers from a long-term debilitating illness, family care can fall apart due to any number of reasons—lifestyle changes, health incidents, and more. And long-term family care can breed resentment and end up making everyone unhappy. So take care of your long-term care issues early, and encourage your parents to do the same. I predict that one day, when all of the baby boomers are drooling in their wheelchairs, this kind of insurance will be as ubiquitous as health care insurance is today.

Pick up a copy of *The Complete Idiot's Guide to Caring for Aging Parents* (Alpha Books, 2001) by Linda Colvin Rhodes for a more complete description of the legal matters surrounding your parents' incapacity planning. Your attorney or your parents' attorney will help you make sure you've covered the important issues, as well. To consider some of the important questions that mark the beginning of this process, however, you can use the Planning for Parents Checklist. Check the items that you can safely answer "yes" to, and help your parents get to work on those unchecked items.

Reducing or Eliminating Estate Taxes

Estate taxes are levied against any estate value that exceeds $2 million dollars. Estate taxes are due, cash on the barrelhead, nine months after the individual's death. It's true that Uncle Sam will grant you a loan and allow you to pay estate taxes over time (with interest, of course). I recommend that you don't accept your dear uncle's offer, and instead plan for reducing or otherwise paying your estate taxes.

Planning for Parents Checklist

☐   Do your parents have current estate documents in place:

- ○ Wills
- ○ Trusts
- ○ Health care powers of attorney
- ○ Durable powers of attorney

☐   Do your parents have long-term care insurance?

☐   Are your parents financially independent?

☐   Are your parents physically capable of caring for themselves?

☐   Do your parents live near you?

☐   Do your parents have a network of family or friends in reasonable proximity to them on a daily basis?

☐   Do you have names and phone numbers for this support network?

☐   Have your parents pre-arranged funerals, burial, or other final wishes?

☐   Do you have access to your parents' important papers and documents?

☐   Have your parents created a list of prescription medications and health care providers for you?

☐   Do your parents need help with home maintenance or bill paying?

☐   Will your parents need special health care assistance in the home?

☐   Will your parents be able to prepare meals?

☐   Do your parents have a personal emergency response system?

The most important thing to remember is that you are likely to get taken to the cleaners by estate taxes if you have assets that aren't easily and quickly converted into cash. Say, for example, that when you're 25, your lovely Auntie Mame leaves you a nice apartment building in Cincinnati. Ten years later, you get run over by a bus. You wrote up a will, however, leaving the building to your young nephew Patrick, the struggling artist. That building is now worth $8 million dollars, which means the estate now owes $2 to $3 million in estate tax before dear Patrick can get possession of the building. Maybe he can borrow against the building with a mortgage, but with his lack of past financial security, he may have trouble getting that loan. Yes, he can take

Uncle Sam's loan, but a better solution would have been a $3 million life insurance policy that you had in place specifically to pay your estate taxes.

The Estate Tax Calculator gives you a down-and-dirty method for estimating your estate taxes. First, you need to determine what your taxable estate value will be, and the IRS gives clear instructions for determining that. The first $2 million isn't counted in 2008, so if your estate is worth $2,040,000, your estate will owe estate tax on $40,000. As the Calculator's chart indicates, the estate tax on $40,000 is $8,200, plus 40 percent of any value above $40,000. Use the Calculator to see what the tax would be in your situation.

	A	B	C	D	E	F	G
1			Estate Tax Calculator				
2			(2008 Rates)				
3							
4							
5	Taxable Estate				Tentative Tax Equals		
6							
7			Taxable		Base		
8	Taxable Amount		Amount Does		Tax		Excess Over
9	Exceeds		Not Exceed		Amount	Plus	Amount
11	$ -	$ 10,000		$ -	18%	$ -
12	$ 10,000	$ 20,000		$ 1,800	20%	$ 10,000
13	$ 20,000	$ 40,000		$ 3,800	22%	$ 20,000
14	$ 40,000	$ 60,000		$ 8,200	24%	$ 40,000
15	$ 60,000	$ 80,000		$ 13,000	26%	$ 60,000
16	$ 80,000	$ 100,000		$ 18,200	28%	$ 80,000
17	$ 100,000	$ 150,000		$ 23,800	30%	$ 100,000
18	$ 150,000	$ 250,000		$ 38,800	32%	$ 150,000
19	$ 250,000	$ 500,000		$ 70,800	34%	$ 250,000
20	$ 500,000	$ 750,000		$ 155,800	37%	$ 500,000
21	$ 750,000	$ 1,000,000		$ 248,300	39%	$ 750,000
22	$ 1,000,000	$ 1,250,000		$ 345,800	41%	$ 1,000,000
23	$ 1,250,000	$ 1,500,000		$ 448,300	43%	$ 1,250,000
24	$ 1,500,000			$ 555,800	45%	$ 1,500,000
25						
26						
27						
28						
29	Your Taxable Estate		$ 160,000			
30	Base Tax Amount		$ 38,800			
32	Excess Over Amount		$ 10,000			
33	Estate Tax Rate		32%			
35	Additional Estate Taxes		$ 3,200			
36						
37	Total Estate Tax		$ 42,000			

You have options for reducing your estate to prevent any need for estate taxes. You can, for example, give property away prior to death to charities, family members, friends, or whomever you choose to shower with your goods. For tax purposes, you're only able to give any one person or charity $12,000 per year without invoking gift taxes. But, you can give that amount to any number of people or organizations every year.

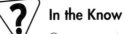

In the Know _____

Go to www.irs.gov to find the government's estate tax rules and an IRS version of the estate tax calculator that uses current tax rates.

If avoiding these taxes is a major concern, congratulations! You should hire an estate tax attorney or a qualified financial planner to help you make the best plan for controlling these taxes.

The Least You Need to Know

- ◆ Making an estate plan isn't just a concern of the wealthy. If you own anything, have any debts, and have any living relatives, you need an estate plan that covers all issues of ownership, distribution, and inheritance.

- ◆ A will is a legal document that determines what happens to your property and dependents after your death. Choosing the beneficiaries and guardians you assign in your will requires careful thought. Review your choices regularly, to make sure they're still adequate.

- ◆ A trust is a legal entity that owns funds or other property managed by an individual or entity (the trustee) for the benefit of another individual or entity (the beneficiary). Trusts are administered by trustees, who follow the trust's guidelines to manage trust disbursements.

- ◆ Incapacity planning outlines your wishes for your care and the care of your property and dependents during any time that you are incapable of providing that care or making those decisions. You and your aging parents should have an incapacity plan in place.

- ◆ The federal government charges estate taxes on any estate valued over $2 million in 2008 with a scheduled increase to $3.5 million in 2009. You have a number of ways to reduce your estate value and avoid these taxes; see an estate tax specialist to create a sound and secure plan.

Chapter 16

When It's Time to Call in the Pros

In This Chapter

- ◆ Deciding that you can't do it all yourself
- ◆ What to consider when working with a financial professional
- ◆ Evaluating your professional needs
- ◆ When you need to choose a new advisor

America started out as a do-it-yourself kind of nation, but these days we're more likely to have a lot of help keeping our lives in order. You might think nothing of paying someone to pedicure your toenails, but still feel that you should be able to make do with a do-it-yourself will form that you found on the Internet. My advice to you is to get over it, and call in a professional when you need one. Most of us can handle some aspect of our financial planning, but all of us need help with some part of it. Protecting your financial future isn't a make do kind of process.

The good news is that there are plenty of good financial advisors out there, and the tools in this chapter will help you determine when you need one, and how to go about choosing a pro who's right for you. The chapter also offers checklists and worksheets to help you evaluate your current professional relationships and transition to a new one, if necessary.

Can You Do It All Yourself?

As a financial professional, I have yet to encounter a situation in which I couldn't offer major improvements over the results my clients could achieve on their own. I can almost always make recommendations that may improve their investment, savings, estate, education, or other financial plan.

Some things you just can't do for yourself, and some financial arrangements you might think of as self-directed, really aren't. Take, for example, buying insurance—an important part of your personal financial plan that you'll purchase from an agent. You might think you're saving money by serving as your own agent and buying insurance online, but in fact, you're still working with a licensed insurance agent who will get a commission from selling you your policy. Now, you might have benefited from all of your online research, but in the end, which agent would you rather have when you actually need to submit an insurance claim? The nameless/faceless person who typed back a response to your online questionnaire, or that flesh and blood person sitting across the desk from you when you signed on the dotted line? And, if you're buying a 20-year term life insurance policy, that flesh and blood agent will probably quote you a price similar to the one you'll find online, anyway.

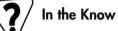

In the Know

If you find insurance policies or other services online for a lower price than a bricks-and-mortar professional is offering, have a discussion with that professional about the price. He or she might be able to explain why the policy they recommend is higher, and perhaps worth the extra price.

Many DIY folks are really careful and do a good job—and I know that you might very well be one of those folks. I advise you, however, to use all of the tools in this chapter to help decide what you can, and can't do to manage your finances. You can start by using the Professional Needs Checklist. Read through every item in the list, then place a checkmark in the appropriate column for those tasks you feel you can do on your own, and those that you feel might better be left to a professional. If you check the DIY column for every task, you need to ask yourself how you became so darned authoritative on all of these incredibly diverse tasks. For those tasks that you have decided to handle on your own, make sure you've read up—in this book and elsewhere—on the responsibilities and processes you'll be undertaking.

	A	B	C	D
1	**Professional Needs Checklist**			
2		**Professional Need**	**DIY**	**Hire a Pro**
3				
4		Cash Flow Analysis		
5		Investment Analysis		
6		Investment Management		
7		Tax Preparation		
8		Estate Planning Documents		
9		Life Insurance Analysis		
10		Life Insurance Purchase		
11		Disability Income Insurance Purchase		
12		Long-Term Care Insurance Purchase		
13		Property and Casualty Insurance Analysis		
14		Buying or Selling a Business		
15		Comprehensive Financial Planning (coordinating all the parts)		
16		Life Planning		
17		Buying or Selling a House		

In this workbook, you can tackle a number of the tasks listed on the Professional Needs Checklist. If you sailed through the process, you're good to go. If you stumbled, however, you might want to rethink your do-it-yourself credentials for that particular financial planning and management process.

Choosing a Financial Professional

Hiring a professional financial advisor isn't as easy as hiring a good auto mechanic. In fact, it's more like finding the right kind of medical specialist to care for your health needs. Here are some points to consider:

♦ You need to be certain that the pro you're using has the specific skills you need. The lawyer who handles your real estate transactions probably isn't the right attorney to handle your estate plan or pending litigation.

♦ You need to be comfortable with your advisor's style. You'll be discussing your finances, health concerns, family relationships, or other highly personal information with these advisors, so their manner, attentiveness, and general attitude will play a big role in how confidentially you are willing to work with them.

♦ You need to get references for any financial advisor you're thinking of working with, just as you would with any professional you were considering hiring. Talk with other clients whose needs are similar to yours. If an advisor doesn't want to give you client names due to confidentiality issues, ask if she can give you the name of other professionals who have worked with her clients, and could pass along what those clients say about her.

Always schedule an initial getting to know you meeting with any professional you're considering. Most professionals should be willing to have those meetings free-of-charge. During the meeting ask questions and take careful notes. Your individual needs may dictate the nature of many of your questions, but the questions listed on the Professional Advisor Questionnaire are relevant for any initial meeting. Use the form to note special information or concerns for any question.

Pitfall Alert!

> If the professional advisor you're meeting with is answering a cell phone and deal-
> ing with frequent interruptions rather than listening to you and asking the right ques-
> tions during your conversation, look elsewhere. If an advisor isn't even interested in your
> concerns as a potential client, you have to wonder how closely that person will focus
> on your goals after he or she gets your business.

As you hire professionals to work with you, make sure you keep a running list of their names and contact information. The Professional Advisors List is a good place to do that. And remember to keep the relevant names from this list with your estate plan, will, and/or other important financial planning documents.

Evaluating Your Existing Professional Relationships

After you've brought a professional on-board, you still can't sit back and assume that everything's okay with your financial life. Sure, you checked all of your pro's references and he passed the initial meeting with flying colors. But then, one day down the road, you might start getting an uncomfortable feeling that something isn't quite right. Maybe he's not returning calls to you as promptly as he used to or giving you the type of follow-through you're accustomed to receiving. Or maybe you just feel that the overall level of attention from this advisor has fallen off.

Because your relationship with a financial advisor is so personal, don't ignore gut feelings that the relationship is going sour. But you don't have to rely on gut instinct alone. Use the Professional Relationship Evaluator to rate a range of professionals on issues such as their technical competency, the reasonableness of their fees, the timeliness of their service, or their willingness to offer advice and direction when you need it. Give each pro an A, B, C, D, or F rating (just like you got in school, with A as your best rating and F as your worst) on each question.

Use the ratings to help determine whether you should meet with a professional to discuss improvements in his or her services or start shopping around for a replacement. You might not want to settle for a pro who earns a C or D rating.

Professional Advisor Questionnaire

1. How long have you been in practice?

_____

_____

2. What credentials have you earned or obtained?

_____

_____

3. What experience do you have in the matters where I need assistance?

_____

_____

4. Do you have any specialty areas of expertise or focus?

_____

_____

5. Will you put your advice in writing?

_____

_____

6. Have you ever been disciplined or had any professional licenses or designations revoked or suspended?

_____

_____

7. Are you a member of any professional associations?

_____

_____

8. How do you stay current on new laws or trends in your area of expertise?

_____

_____

9. What professional licenses do you hold?

_____

_____

continues

208 **Part 4:** Planning for the Future

continued

10. What can you tell me about your firm?

_____

_____

11. How do you get paid?

_____

_____

12. Will you disclose the nature, frequency, and amount of your compensation to me?

_____

_____

13. How many clients do you serve?

_____

_____

14. What is the ideal client profile for you?

_____

_____

15. What are the characteristics of your average client?

_____

_____

16. Do you work with a specific team of other professionals outside of your firm?

_____

_____

17. May I speak to your clients—people just like me who use your services?

_____

_____

	A	B	C	D	E
1			Professional Advisors List		
2					
3	Type of Advisor	Name	Address	Phone #	E-Mail Address
4					
5	Attorney				
6	Accountant				
7	Financial Planner				
8	Investment Advisor				
9	Insurance				
10	Banker				
11	Mortgage Broker				
12	Employee Benefits Advisor				

A	B	C	D	E	F	G	H	I
1	Professional Relationship Evaluator							
2	Evaluation Criteria	CPA	Attorney	Insurance Agent	Investment Professional	Benefits Consultant	Realtor	Other
3								
4	Technical competency							
5	Personality							
6	Returns calls promptly							
7	Reasonableness of fees							
8	Proactively looks out for my needs							
9	Works well with other advisors							
10	Available when needed							
11	Personal attention							
12	Timeliness of services							
13	Empathy and care							
14	Accuracy							
15	Understands my needs							
16	Listens to me							
17	Gives advice and direction							

Hiring a New Professional Financial Advisor

If you decide that it's time to switch financial pros, don't worry. It's not that tough to do. Most of the work you'll do with an estate attorney, investment advisor, insurance agent, or other financial planning professional is relatively portable to another individual or agency. As a financial advisor, I take over other advisor's accounts all the time. In fact, sometimes it's easier working with clients who have been through the process before, and have a better idea of what they want (and don't want) from our relationship. Switching advisors may be more difficult for you than the professional you're leaving, but don't let that stop you. This is business, remember.

Pitfall Alert!

Don't let price be the guiding factor in choosing a financial professional. Every professional makes a profit, so you just have to ask yourself if someone who charges a fifth of the going rate is earning his or her living by selling clients stuff they don't need, or shorting them on other services. When it comes to financial management, a bargain-rate professional is frequently not a bargain.

If you're ready to make the change, whip out your Professional Advisor Questionnaire, and restart your search process. Before you head off to your initial meeting, however, tick through the questions on the Advisor Change Checklist to make sure you have all of the information you'll need in your meeting and that you've thought over issues your potential advisor may want to discuss.

Advisor Change Checklist

☐   Do you have copies of all relevant documents, etc.?

☐   Will the former professional cooperate during the transition?

☐   How will you inform the former advisor?

☐   Can files be transferred electronically?

☐   Are there any exit fees or costs to leave the former advisor?

☐   Are there any outstanding invoices or fees owed to the former advisor?

☐   Is there any unfinished business or work in progress with the former advisor?

The Least You Need to Know

- Everyone can benefit from guidance with some part of their financial planning and management process. Get the professional help you need so your plan is complete, accurate, legal, and effective.

- Treat a financial professional as you would anyone whose services you're contracting. Make sure the individual listens to your concerns and gives your concerns the attention needed.

- If you feel that you are no longer getting the service you need, explore the problem with your advisor, and if it can't be fixed, be prepared to replace that advisor.

- When hiring a new professional, make sure everything is in order for the transition and vet the professional carefully.

Glossary

In the course of this book, you've encountered a number of terms that might have been unfamiliar (or unimportant) to you before you started thinking about managing your personal finances. This glossary offers definitions for many of those terms, along with some others you might encounter when using any of the publications, websites, and other resources mentioned in this book.

401K   A type of employer-sponsored retirement plan that allows an employee to save for retirement while deferring taxes on the saved money and earnings until it is withdrawn.

accrued interest   Interest that has been earned but not received.

adjusted gross estate   The adjusted gross estate is equal to the gross estate less any deductions for funeral expenses, last medical expenses, administrative expenses, debts, and losses during the administration of an estate.

adjusted gross income (AGI)   The amount of all the money you earned in a given year, minus allowable adjustments.

after-tax yield   The rate of interest you receive on an investment after taxes have been calculated and subtracted.

AGI   *See* adjusted gross income.

annuity   A contract or agreement in which a person invests in a tax-deferred environment and may receive fixed payments on an investment for a lifetime or for a specified number of years. *See also* fixed annuity; variable annuity.

asset   Anything owned by an individual or business that has commercial exchange value. *See also* financial asset; liquid asset.

balanced funds   Mutual funds whose underlying investments are a blend of stocks and bonds.

blue-chip stocks   Stocks of well-established companies such as General Electric, Exxon Mobil, and so on.

bond   An interest-bearing certificate that is issued by a business or government, promising to pay the holder a specified amount on a specified date.

budget   A plan for allocating your net income, ideally in a way that enables you to meet all outside financial obligations as well as your personal financial/savings goals and objectives.

cash flow   The money that enters your control as income and leaves your accounts as expenditures.

cash journal   A written record of your out-of-pocket expenses, which you might keep over a period of weeks or a month in order to determine where you're spending the cash you carry with you.

cash-surrender value (CSV)   The amount of money an insured will receive if he or she cancels an insurance policy that carries this option—typically, a whole-life, universal life, or variable life insurance plan. *See also* whole-life insurance.

certificate of deposit (CD)   A bank savings vehicle which will pay a specified interest rate on your deposited funds at a specified maturity date.

closed-end lease   An automobile lease that enables you to return your vehicle at the end of the lease period. *See also* open-end lease.

closing costs   Fees charged by a lender for surveys, property taxes, title insurance, and other required activities necessary to legally complete the transfer of a home's ownership.

co-pay   A set amount an insured individual must pay for every doctor's visit or other medical event in addition to the payment the insurance company makes for that event.

commodities   Metals, oil, and other material assets that are bought and traded on the open market.

compounded interest   Interest not only on your original deposit, but also on the accumulated interest that deposit earns over time.

consumer debt   Debt that is accumulated primarily through the purchase of consumer goods, which means the interest payments charged for this debt are not tax deductible (as is mortgage debt and other secured debts).

contingency planning   Your plan for meeting the costs of expenses that may occur at some unknown time in the near future—such as insurance deductibles and co-pays or the replacement of a car that's near the end of its useful life.

credit history   A record of an individual's borrowing and repayment behavior that includes current debt load, past bankruptcies, and so on. *See also* credit rating; credit score.

credit rating   A ranking number that credit bureaus assign to an individual based on the agency's analysis of that individual's credit history; lenders use this number to determine the individual's ability to meet debt obligations. A higher credit rating means better chances of being approved for a loan.

credit report   A detailed collection of information identifying an individual and profiling his or her credit history that credit reporting agencies sell to lenders to enable those lenders to determine whether the individual is an acceptable credit risk.

credit score   A credit rating assigned by FICO (Fair Isaac Corporation) that ranges between 300 and 850. Many lenders determine whether to loan you money and what interest rate to charge you based on this score. *See also* FICO.

death benefit   An amount of money paid by Social Security or an insurer to a deceased insured's beneficiaries.

debt consolidation plan   A plan devised by a credit counseling agency to incorporate all of an individual's outstanding debt payments into a single payment, typically at a lower interest rate than the individual is currently paying.

debt load   The total amount of debt an individual currently owns. *See also* unsecured debt; secured debt.

deductible   A portion of claim costs the insured must pay before the insurance company will make any payment toward those claim costs.

disability insurance   Insurance coverage for replacing some of the insured's regular income, should the insured suffer a disability that leaves him/her unable to perform regular work duties.

down payment   An amount of money that a lender requires you to pay toward the costs of purchasing a home, car, or other property for which you are borrowing funds.

durable power of attorney   The legal authority to handle another person's personal, financial, medical, and legal affairs—often assigned by aging parents to an adult child. These rights continue on, even when the person who assigned those rights becomes physically or mentally incapacitated.

equity   *See* stock.

equity loan   An advance of money that a lender extends to you, using for collateral the value you have accumulated in your home or some other asset. Home-equity loans often are called second mortgages.

executor   The person you appoint to carry out the provisions of your will.

expense ratio   The percent of the investor's money that the fund's management uses each year to run the fund. Typical expense ratios are between 1 and 1.5 percent.

Fair Isaac Corporation   *See* FICO.

fee-for-service   A medical insurance plan in which the insured pays a percentage of his or her medical service fees, after meeting his or her deductible.

FICO   The acronym for Fair Isaac Corporation, the creator of the most widely used credit score model in the United States. A person's FICO score is calculated using information from his or her credit history.

fiduciaries   The people or institutions you appoint to specific roles in your estate plan, trust, or will.

financial asset   An asset that can be sold or traded in for cash. *See also* liquid asset.

financial goal   A broad financial purpose toward which you're working, such as owning a home, having a financially comfortable retirement, or eliminating credit card debt.

financial instrument   A contract or other written document that has monetary value or records a financial transaction.

financial liability   A contractual obligation to pay cash or some other financial asset to another person or business under conditions that may be unfavorable to you.

financial objective   A plan of action designed to achieve a financial goal, such as setting up and contributing to a savings plan designed to accrue a specific amount of money by a specific date, to pay for a planned vacation.

fixed annuities   Annuities that offer a set interest rate and the potential for a series of equal payouts over a fixed period of time. *See also* variable annuities.

fund manager   The person or team responsible for managing a fund's holdings.

goal   The broad purpose you're working toward. *See also* objective.

growth stocks   Stocks of companies whose mission is to grow by exploring new markets, products, or other opportunities.

guardian   Someone you've appointed to care for you while incapacitated or your minor dependents.

hedge funds   Pools of money that are exempt from most rules and regulations that govern other mutual funds. They typically use a lot of aggressive strategies to accomplish their investing goals and often have minimum investment amounts and holding periods.

homeowner's insurance   Insurance that covers the costs of specified types of damage to the insured's dwelling, possessions, and in many cases, losses resulting from accidents, injuries, and legal actions associated with insured property.

individual retirement account (IRA)   A retirement plan that allows a contributor to pay a limited yearly amount toward retirement, while deferring taxes on the interest earned in the account. Types include Roth and traditional IRAs.

international funds   Mutual funds whose underlying holdings are in foreign investment.

intestate   The legal term for someone who dies without a will.

investment real estate   Real estate that is not your primary residence and that you purchased for the purpose of generating income or capital gains.

itemized deductions   Expenses that the Internal Revenue Service code allows you to claim on your individual income tax return and then subtract from your adjusted gross income. *See also* adjusted gross income (AGI).

liability coverage   Insurance coverage that stipulates the insurer will pay the costs of legal liability, often including legal defense costs for personal or property damage involving the named insured.

liquid asset   An asset that involves funds—such as cash, checks, stocks, bonds, life insurance with cash-surrender value, IRAs, other retirement funds, and so on—that can be cashed in quickly in exchange for cash. *See also* financial asset.

living will   A document that sets forth your wishes for administering your finances, estate, and health care wishes should you become incapacitated for some period of time before your death.

load funds   Mutual funds that pay commissions to brokers. *See also* no-load funds.

long-term care insurance   A type of insurance that helps provide for the cost of long-term care beyond a specified period.

loss-of-use coverage   Insurance term that stipulates the insurer will cover many temporary costs incurred by the insured as a result of losing the use of insured property (hotel charges, rental cars, and so on).

managed care plan   A medical insurance plan in which the insurer limits the insured's ability to seek medical services at will, and instead requires the insured to use health service providers within the insurer's network of approved and/or preferred providers.

market value   The price which a willing buyer is willing to pay a willing seller for real estate, securities, or other assets in the current marketplace.

maturity date   The date when a loan will be repaid by the borrower.

money-market fund   A type of mutual fund that invests in short-term securities such as Treasury bills and negotiable certificates of deposit. *See also* mutual funds.

mortgage   A loan agreement in which you contract to repay money that you have borrowed in order to secure real estate or other specified property; usually these loans are secured by the specified property item.

mutual funds   A collection of diversified securities such as stocks and bonds, that are purchased and managed for investors by a regulated investment company.

net income   The total amount of money you have coming in each month, minus the amount of money you spend each month. Net income can include cash gifts, wages, sales commissions, bonuses, investment earnings, and business or rental income.

net worth   Your net worth is the total value of your financial assets, minus the total value of your financial liabilities. Your net worth offers a snapshot of your current financial state. *See also* financial asset; financial liability.

no-load funds   Mutual funds with no commissions. *See also* load funds.

NTF (No Transaction Fee)   Mutual funds that can be bought in brokerage accounts without incurring transaction fees.

objective   A specific step toward achieving a goal. *See also* goal.

open-end lease   An automobile lease that, in some cases, requires the person leasing the vehicle to pay at the end of the lease period the difference between the car's current market value and the projected value the dealer assigned to it when the lease was signed. *See also* closed-end lease; residual value.

password protection software   A computer program designed to help you safely store and track passwords used to access accounts and other secured information.

permanent life insurance   A life insurance plan that accumulates a cash value that may be available to the insured while the insured is still living.

points   A lump sum amount of interest some mortgage lenders charge up front, which can lower the loan's interest rate. Each point is 1 percent of the total loan amount.

powers of appointment   Powers that give an individual the right to decide how to distribute another person's property. These powers are typically assigned in wills, trusts, and other legal documents of ownership.

preexisting condition   Any medical condition for which an individual has been treated during a period of time prior to enrollment in a health-care program—a time determined by the insurer.

private mortgage insurance (PMI)   Insurance that protects lenders against losses resulting when borrowers default on their loans. Many lenders require borrowers to carry this insurance when they have put up less than 20 percent of a home's cost as a down payment.

prospectus   A formal written disclosure document that describes the securities and security management plan a business or institution is offering for investor purchase or participation.

renter's insurance   Insurance coverage for an individual's personal possessions and liability associated with accidents and injuries occurring on or involving the insured's rented or leased place of residence. *See also* liability coverage.

replacement cost   A homeowner's or renter's insurance term that stipulates the company will pay the full cost of replacing an item with a new one of similar quality.

residual value   In relation to an automobile lease, the value the dealership determines to represent the price of a leased vehicle at the end of its lease period.

savings vehicle   An account used specifically to accumulate savings.

second mortgage   *See* equity loan.

Section 72t distributions   Funds withdrawn from a traditional or Roth IRA that are designated as premature withdrawals and subject to income tax, but exempt from early withdrawal fines of 10 percent of the amount of the distribution, as stated in Section 72t of the IRS code.

sector funds   Funds that buy only companies in a specific industry, such as technology or health care.

secured credit card   A credit card that gives you access to funds that you have deposited with the company issuing the card.

secured debt   Debt tied to collateral such as a home, business, or other financial asset. If you fail to repay a secured debt, the lender can take ownership of the property you've offered as collateral. *See also* unsecured debt.

separate accounts   In life insurance or annuity contracts, accounts that function similarly to mutual funds. Separate accounts can include stocks, bonds, or any other investment type.

shares   *See* stock.

stock   A type of security in which the holder has ownership in a corporation. Common stock usually entitles the owner the right to vote at shareholder meetings and receive dividends. Preferred stock generally does not allow the owner to vote at shareholder meetings, but it has a higher claim on assets and earnings than the common shares.

target funds   Also known as lifecycle funds or target maturity funds, these funds are targeted and managed for maximum benefit at a specific time period in the future, such as retirement.

tax bracket   A range of income that determines what percentage of an individual's income that individual must pay in income tax.

tax credit   Sums a taxpayer can subtract directly from the amount of tax that individual owes, offered as incentives for any number of actions the taxing agency (federal or state government) wants to encourage, such as saving energy or paying for an education.

tax-deferred investments   Investments such as individual retirement accounts (IRAs) that are not taxed until the investor withdraws and takes possession of the money.

tax-free investments Investments such as municipal bonds where interest is not subject to taxation (tax-exempt).

taxable income An individual's AGI, minus personal exemptions and standard or itemized deductions. It is the net amount on which your income tax is based. *See also* adjusted gross income (AGI).

term life insurance A life insurance plan that pays a benefit when you die and accumulates no cash-surrender value.

trailing performance The past returns or losses of a fund, as calculated on an annual basis.

trustee A person or institution who manages any trusts you establish. The trustee is a fiduciary.

umbrella liability coverage Insurance coverage for liability losses above the limit of regular liability coverage.

uninsured/underinsured motorist coverage Insurance reimbursement for repairs if the insured's vehicle is struck by an uninsured motorist, or when an at-fault driver has insufficient insurance coverage to pay for the insured's total loss, or when the insured is struck as a pedestrian.

universal life insurance An insurance plan that offers a cash accumulation feature for those insured who pay more than the required minimum premiums.

unsecured debt A debt, such as credit card debt, that is not tied to an item of property or other material collateral. *See also* secured debt.

value stocks Stocks deemed undervalued relative to other similar stocks or the company's operating profits or asset base.

variable annuities Annuities in which the holder may select from a wide array of separate or sub accounts that mirror performance of a mutual fund. *See also* fixed annuities.

variable universal life insurance An insurance plan that places the insured's cash value accumulation in a series of separate accounts of the insured's choosing.

vested equity Savings or stock that is fully available to you within your employer's 401K plan, company stock ownership program, or other employee savings and investment plan. Most such plans require that you remain employed with the company providing the plan for a specific period of time—usually years—before you are fully vested and thus have access to the full equity of your account.

whole-life insurance   A type of life insurance designed to be held by the insured throughout his or her life. Cash accumulations in these plans earn a fixed interest rate, and the policy may have a cash-surrender value. *See also* cash-surrender value.

yield   The rate of return to the owner of a security generated from a stock in the form of dividends, or the effective rate of interest paid on a bond.

yield to maturity   All of the returns you realize from a bond since its purchase. *See also* bond.

Resources

There's no shortage of information on financial planning, and the array of books and websites out there can be dizzying. If you want to learn more about the topics covered in this book, the following resources are great places to start.

Books

Budgeting

Feinberg, Margaret, and Natalie Nichols Gillespie. *Five-Star Living on a Two-Star Budget: Living Big on Only a Little*. Harvest House Publishers, 2006.

Lim, Sylvia S. *Personal Budgeting Kit*. Self-Counsel Press, 2005.

Sander, Peter J., and Jennifer Basye Sander. *The Pocket Idiot's Guide to Living on a Budget, Second Edition*. Alpha Books, 2005.

Education Planning

Higgins, Tim. *Pay for College Without Sacrificing Your Retirement: A Guide to Your Financial Future*. Bay Tree Publishing, 2008.

Lipphardt, Debra. *The Scholarship & Financial Aid Solution: How to Go to College for Next to Nothing with Short Cuts, Tricks, and Tips from Start to Finish.* Atlantic Publishing Company, 2008.

Rye, David. *The Complete Idiot's Guide to Financial Aid for College, Second Edition.* Alpha Books, 2008.

Estate Planning

Kraemer, Sandy F. *60-Minute Estate Planner: Fast and Easy Plans for Saving Taxes, Avoiding Probate, and Maximizing Inheritance.* AMACOM, 2006.

Maple, Stephen. *The Complete Idiot's Guide to Wills and Estates, Fourth Edition.* Alpha Books, 2009.

Palermo, Michael T., and Ric Edelman. *AARP Crash Course in Estate Planning: The Essential Guide to Wills, Trusts, and Your Personal Legacy.* Sterling, 2008.

Insurance

Lankford, Kimberly. *The Insurance Maze: How You Can Save Money on Insurance—and Still Get the Coverage You Need.* Kaplan Business, 2006.

Pletzke, Jonathan. *Get a Good Deal on Your Health Insurance Without Getting Ripped-Off.* Aji Publishing, 2007.

Steuer, Anthony. *Questions and Answers on Life Insurance: The Life Insurance Toolbook.* iUniverse Star, 2007.

Personal Finance

Bachrach, Bill. *Values-Based Financial Planning: The Art of Creating and Inspiring Financial Strategy.* Aim High Pub., 2000.

Eisenberg, Lee. *The Number: What Do You Need for the Rest of Your Life and What Will It Cost?* Free Press, 2006.

Fisher, Sarah Young, and Susan Shelly. *The Complete Idiot's Guide to Personal Finance in Your 20s & 30s, Fourth Edition.* Alpha Books, 2009.

Kinder, George. *The Seven Stages of Money Maturity: Understanding the Spirit and Value of Money in Your Life.* Dell, 2000.

Napolitano, John P. The *Complete Idiot's Guide to Success as a Personal Financial Planner.* Alpha Books, 2007.

Needleman, Jacob. *Money and the Meaning of Life.* Doubleday Business, 1994.

Sanduski, Steve, and Ron Carson. *Avalanche: The 9 Principles for Uncovering True Wealth.* Kaplan Publishing, 2007.

Reducing Your Debt

Clark, Ken. *The Complete Idiot's Guide to Getting Out of Debt.* Alpha Books, 2009.

Epstein, Lita. *The Complete Idiot's Guide to Improving Your Credit Score.* Alpha Books, 2007.

Newman, Michael W. *What You Can Do to Conquer Your Credit and Debt Problems.* CreateSpace, 2007.

Warren, Harvey Z. *Forever in Your Debt: Escaping Credit Card Hell.* BookSurge Publishing, 2007.

Retirement

Bolles, Richard Nelson, and John E. Nelson. *What Color Is Your Parachute? for Retirement: Planning Now for the Life You Want.* Ten Speed Press, 2007.

Lane, Jennifer. *The Complete Idiot's Guide to Protecting Your 401(k) and IRA.* Alpha Books, 2009.

Ruffenach, Glenn, and Kelly Greene. *The Wall Street Journal. Complete Retirement Guidebook: How to Plan It, Live It and Enjoy It.* Three Rivers Press, 2007.

Saving and Investing

DeSalvo, Debra, Edward T. Koch, and Joshua Kennon. *The Complete Idiot's Guide to Investing, Third Edition.* Alpha Books, 2006.

Kansas, Dave. *The Wall Street Journal. Complete Money & Investing Guidebook.* Three Rivers Press, 2005.

Morris, Virginia B., and Kenneth M. Morris. *Standard and Poor's Guide to Money and Investing.* McGraw-Hill, 2005.

Taxes

Botkin, Sandy. *Lower Your Taxes—Big Time! 2007–2008 Edition*. McGraw-Hill, 2006.

Fishman, Stephen. *Deduct It! Lower Your Small Business Taxes, Fourth Edition*. NOLO, 2007.

Working with Financial Planners

Davis, Robin S. *Who's Sitting on Your Nest Egg? Why You Need a Financial Advisor and Ten Easy Tests for Finding the Best One*. Bridgeway Books, 2007.

Parisse, Alan, and David Richman. *Questions Great Financial Advisors Ask ... and Investors Need to Know*. Kaplan Business, 2006.

Websites

http://johnnapolitano.org   Website about the author.

www.aarp.org   Website of the American Association of Retired Persons. Click the Money tab for retirement planning resources, including mortgage payoff and nest egg calculators.

www.angieslist.com   Find service companies and health care professionals in your area and review them before you hire them.

www.bbb.org   Better Business Bureau. Look up businesses in your area.

www.billsavings.com   Get tips and tools on managing personal finance, credit and debt, and more.

www.collegeboard.com   Find information on financial aid, scholarships, and more.

www.compuquotes.com   Compare rates on auto insurance, homeowner's and renter's insurance, life insurance, health insurance, and more.

www.fafsa.ed.gov   Fill out a FAFSA (Free Application for Federal Student Aid) and check the status of your application.

www.flamingoworld.com   Get online coupons and discounts for all kinds of merchandise from top stores and websites.

www.fpanet.org   Website of the Financial Planning Association. Choose a financial planner, find articles and tips on financial planning, participate in online discussions.

www.ftc.gov   Website of the Federal Trade Commission. Find information about national consumer protection laws.

www.healthinsuranceinfo.net   Find your state's health insurance rules and guidelines.

www.hud.gov   Website of the U.S. Department of Housing and Urban Development. Find information and services, including buying HUD homes, avoiding foreclosure, buying and selling a home, and more.

www.ira.com   Get information on what IRA is right for you.

www.irs.gov   Website of the Internal Revenue Service. Find answers to frequently asked questions about taxes, learn about tax credits, download tax forms, and much more.

www.kiplinger.com   Get advice on personal finances and investments, use financial management tools and calculators.

www.morningstar.com   Get the latest information on the performance of mutual funds, order a prospectus, and more.

www.mortgage.com   Find information about mortgages, rates, refinancing options, and more.

www.nfcc.org   Website of the National Foundation for Credit Counseling. Get consumer debt advice, find links to credit counseling agencies, bankruptcy information, and more.

www.pmi-US.com/rates   Look up current Private Mortgage Insurance rates.

www.practicalmoneyskills.com   Find tips, newsletters, and calculators designed to help you practice better money management skills.

www.rothira.com   Get information about Roth 401K plans, including articles, tips, and calculators.

www.savingforcollege.com   Set up a 529 plan, consult with financial experts, use calculators, and more.

www.savingsbonds.gov   Purchase and manage Treasury securities.

www.smartmoney.com   Get investment advice, real-time stock market quotes, advice on managing elder finances, saving for college, retirement, and more.

www.ssa.gov Website of the Social Security Administration. Check on your projected benefits, apply for disability and retirement benefits, and more.

www.staffordloan.com Apply online for a federal Stafford Student Loan (SSL).

Index

Check out these

BEST-SELLERS

READ BY MILLIONS!

FULL COLOR!

978-1-59257-115-4
$16.95

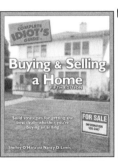

978-1-59257-458-2
$19.95

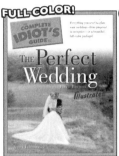

978-1-59257-566-4
$22.95

978-1-59257-485-8
$24.95

978-1-59257-480-3
$19.95

978-1-59257-469-8
$14.95

978-1-59257-439-1
$18.95

978-1-59257-483-4
$14.95

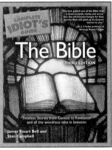

978-1-59257-389-9
$18.95

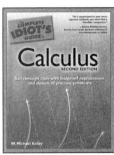

978-1-59257-471-1
$18.95

978-1-59257-437-7
$19.95

978-1-59257-463-6
$14.95

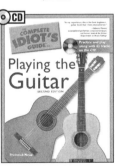

978-0-02864244-4
$21.95

978-1-59257-335-6
$19.95

978-1-59257-491-9
$19.95

More than **450 titles** available at booksellers and online retailers everywhere

ALPHA

www.idiotsguides.com